# THE **EIGHT**
## **PRINCIPLES** OF
# **SUSTAINABLE**
# **FUNDRAISING**

**TRANSFORMING
FUNDRAISING
ANXIETY INTO THE
OPPORTUNITY OF
A LIFETIME**

## Larry C Johnson, CFRE

The Eight Principles of Sustainable Fundraising:
Transforming Fundraising Anxiety into the Opportunity of a Lifetime
by Larry C. Johnson

For general information on other Eight Principles™ products and services, email larry@megraceassociates.com or see TheEightPrinciples.com.

To purchase copies of Eight Principles book or workbook in large quantities at wholesale prices, please contact Aloha Publishing at alohapublishing@gmail.com.

Cover design: Cari Campbell, Cari Campbell Design
Interior layout: Nick Zelinger, NZ Graphics

ISBN: 978-1-61206-022-4

Library of Congress Control Number: 2011940529

First Printing

Printed in Canada

Published by:
AlohaPublishing.com

ALOHA
PUBLISHING

*To Connie, for her loving patience and support*

# Contents

# Transforming Fundraising Anxiety

B eing asked to fundraise for a worthy charity or cause engenders both desire and fear—desire to be successful in something you believe in, while being fearful that you're not up to the task or will even be rejected by those you solicit. If you have a similar reaction, rest assured—you're in good company.

I once worked with a board member of a nonprofit organization who, by his personality and background, appeared to be virtually fearless. A Marine officer decorated for service in combat, he was also a successful businessman with his own engineering firm and stood six feet, three inches tall and ramrod straight. Having made a substantial gift in the fundraising campaign on which he was working, he was eager to ask others to join him. He approached an elderly dowager in the community, known to be both generous and demanding. When he asked her for a gift, her response was, "David, look me in the eye when you ask me for that kind of money." Confronted with the task of actually asking, he had apparently lost his nerve. It doesn't have to be that way.

When you hear the word "fundraising," what comes to mind? You may think of the endless appeals for funds that appear in the mail or—don't we love this—the well-timed telephone solicitor's call right at dinner. Responding to seemingly endless invitations to fundraising events, from charity auctions to golfing outings, you may openly wonder, "Isn't there a better way to do this?" In a word, yes. That "better way" is the straightforward set of principles described in the upcoming chapters. These principles, taken together and implemented consistently, will achieve the sustainable philanthropic revenue you are seeking for your organization. Seeking gifts for a worthy charitable undertaking should be one of the most rewarding and uplifting activities in which you'll ever participate. Let me say that again. Seeking gifts for a worthy charitable organization or undertaking should be one of the most rewarding and uplifting activities in which you'll ever participate.

Let's look at a hypothetical scenario. A well-informed volunteer—perhaps someone you know—approaches you on behalf of a worthwhile organization or charitable cause. During your conversation, she seeks to find how this organization and its work might resonate with your personal values and satisfy a deep-felt need for involvement with the "greater good," to do something truly lasting and worthwhile, perhaps even leave a legacy. The volunteer then seeks to enlist your support by asking you to become a partner with the organization's leadership, thereby realizing goals that you, yourself, deem worthy. Once you've committed, if the organization keeps your faith by keeping you informed and involved, while earnestly soliciting your feedback, you're likely to become a long-term, if not lifetime, partner. That's sustainable fundraising. Fundraising that is sustainable, even expandable, isn't really about money. It's about building partnerships between your organization and its donors, partnerships that are built upon mutually beneficial goals.

Unfortunately, few nonprofit organizations see their donors as investors—partners whose goals and aims are as important as the organization's. Most nonprofit organizations, almost out of necessity if nothing else, are on a figurative "raise money treadmill," always scrambling to fund their operations and programmatic outreach in what seems to be a never-ending struggle. By making money the object, rather than relationships, nonprofits fall into a trap—the same trap Jim Collins alluded to when he stated that money is an input of a nonprofit but not an output.[1] The outputs, according to Collins, are life-changing outcomes that touch both giver and receiver. Being efficient

---

[1] Collins, Jim. *Good to Great and the Social Sectors.* 2005. 4ff.

is not the goal, being effective is. Organizations such as Teach for America and Habitat for Humanity understand this truth and have well-funded and successful fundraising programs that possess both an adequate internal infrastructure and a focus on relationships. As a result, both organizations continue to enjoy healthy bottom lines in their fundraising programs, year after year.

Growth, in both scope and sophistication, of the fundraising profession and industry hasn't done very much to encourage nonprofit organizations to view their donors as investors or serious partners. This is not to say professional fundraising hasn't been of immense benefit to our charitable organizations. Philanthropy in the United States has experienced tremendous growth during the past forty years or so, when good data became available. Some of this increase is undoubtedly due to the growth of professional development programs in nonprofit organizations. What professional development has brought us is the development system: a collection of fundraising programs in a given charitable organization that, taken together, approach various types of donors seeking gifts through varied vehicles and appeals. Some organizational development systems allow for donors to "mature" in their support of the organization over the donors' lifetimes ("moves management," for example) and a few even seriously encourage giving based upon a particular interest within the organization. What's missing here is not so much the "how" as the "why."

When the focus is on the "how" in fundraising, raising money becomes a process that manages commodities for inputs and outputs. Donors become cogs in a machine—or worse—resources merely to be mined. When the focus is on the "why" in fundraising, donors become participants integral to the effective outcomes for which the organization is striving; they become investors who are fully engaged in the organization.

Fundraising professionals themselves often contribute, sometimes unwittingly, to an organizational emphasis on "program driven" fundraising, which is driven by organizational initiatives. When fundraisers are evaluated primarily using cash-based or activity-related criteria, they develop, quite naturally, a "month-to-month" or "quarter-to-quarter" focus. The cash driven mindset can put fundraisers from the same organization in competition for the same donors, leading to donor confusion, fatigue or outright disgust.

By and large, even with the growing number of charitable organizations in the United States and increased sophistication in the fundraising profession, most organizations have, at best, a "program delivery" mindset as they reach out to their potential supporters. It's the classic inside-out, "push" marketing approach that for-profit companies have used, quite effectively, for decades. Businesses have only recently discovered the extraordinary power and leverage of "pull" or "permission marketing." This approach seeks to engage prospective customers by learning about them and drawing them in first, before seeking a sale, rather than "pushing" out internally designed and approved "products" for their consumption. In this regard, charitable organizations have the intrinsic advantage over the for-profit company…if they choose to use it. Charitable organizations, by their very nature, provide an intangible, but quite powerful, incentive for donors to invest. It's the opportunity for true self-fulfillment, a legacy and the experience of a lifetime—participation in something truly greater than themselves.

Adopting a sustainable approach to your organization's fundraising is more about embracing basic attitudes and practices and being consistent with these rather than how much money you spend on fundraising. Make no mistake; fundraising does require a financial investment. Your organization needs to be prepared for this. It is, however, just that: an investment—the financial return is greater, often far greater, than the cost. That's as it should be. In fact, sustainable fundraising programs are far lower in cost than those based largely upon transactions.[2] For fundraising to be successful over time, a proper infrastructure must be present and a long-term financial investment made. Without these, even the most well-intentioned fundraising efforts will net largely that—good intentions. That being said, it is not money or the expertise of your staff that will ultimately achieve true sustainable, expandable success. It is the adoption and consistent application of the principles that I have chosen to call "The Eight Principles of Sustainable Fundraising™."

There is nothing fundamentally new or radically different about any of these principles. Fundraising professionals, especially those of us who have been practicing for a while, may recognize the ideas behind these principles as just "good fundraising" or even "common sense." All true. But as Voltaire discovered some time ago, "common sense is not so common." Many charitable organizations already follow one, two or even three or more of these principles, at least to some degree. It is in the adoption, however, of all eight of these principles into the culture of the organization that creates true transformation.

Fundraising is ultimately about people—people investing in the lives of others. Regardless of how sophisticated our work becomes with statistical matrixes, behavioral models and excursions into sociology, person-to-person will always be the essential paradigm. In the over two decades I have been privileged to work with donors, I have strived to never forget that fact.

Developing a dependable, renewable and even expandable stream of fundraising revenue is possible for all organizations, small and

---

[2] The average direct costs of event fundraising ranges between $0.50 and $0.75 per dollar raised, while the cost range for a comprehensive program using sustainable principles is between $0.18 and $0.25 per dollar raised.

large—achieving this is what is known as "sustainable fundraising." It's within your organization's reach. Yes, I think you have it now: it's not about money, it's about people.

# Giving Yourself the Opportunity
## of a Lifetime

Rather than the stress-producing undertaking it often is, raising funds for a cause or organization you believe in can be—and should be, as I previously stated—one of the most rewarding and personally satisfying endeavors you will ever undertake.

Although there is both a science and an art to the process, successful fundraising—fundraising which generates sustainable philanthropic revenue—is based upon a set of straightforward, uncomplicated principles. These principles, though simple, must be taken as a whole and executed consistently over time. Understanding and applying this system does not require the foresight of a prophet, the intellect of a physicist or the resources of a billionaire. It does require a steadfast belief in the cause being pursued and a bit of tenaciousness—qualities that are in abundance among the supporters of most nonprofit organizations.

Building a program of sustainable fundraising requires a strong and vibrant outreach to individual donors. That's not to say corporate giving and foundation grants aren't possible or should be ignored; it's simply recognizing the fact that the vast majority of philanthropic gifts are made by individuals, rather than corporations or large foundation grants. This is counter to what many people in the not-for-profit, high impact world of tax-exempt organizations believe.

But the statistics do not lie. Living individuals consistently account for about 75 percent of the roughly $300 billion that is given to philanthropy in the United States each year. Bequests account for another 8 percent or so. Although foundations currently provide about 12 percent of the funds, half of those foundations are *family* foundations; hence, they look and act more as individuals than their independent counterparts. Gifts from individuals, then, account for almost 90 percent of all the charitable giving in the U.S. What's more, corporate gifts and foundation grants are less flexible with regard to how the funds can be used and have a far lower renewal rate than gifts given by individuals.

It takes willing and able individuals to successfully engage and solicit potential donors. Each year, tens of thousands of individuals in the United States become volunteers and accept leadership positions in charitable organizations for the very first time, hoping to do just that. They offer their time and talent while bristling with enthusiasm. The ranks of professional fundraisers continue to grow each year, as well, for many of the same reasons. But all of the well-intentioned energy these men and women bring to their tasks is often dampened when they are confronted with the reality of the need to raise funds for their respective causes—significant funds, often rapidly. Discouragement, even disso-lution, can quickly set in. For, as individuals volunteer for nonprofits and new professional fundraisers are minted at a healthy pace, many of those same men and women will drop out almost as fast.

Why? To many of those who are on the "outside" (and even some on the inside) fundraising for charitable organizations is viewed as either (1) a monumental quest to successfully navigate the complexities and nuances of endless events, solicitations, grants and trust agreements, or (2) a lifelong search for the lost land of universal donors. In a truly sustainable, even expandable fundraising system, the ideal donors—the donors you want—are investors who expect, demand and deserve a return on their investment in your organization. Philanthropic in-vestors will continue to support your organization through thick and thin; their lifetime impact upon an organization is huge. They are never merely sometimes-purveyors of cash or other assets or prospects from whom gifts are to be solicited. The philanthropic investor is not looking for a financial return, as in the for-profit world, but a return that provides for the fulfillment of his or her deeply held, personal values. These investors want to see tangible outcomes that engage them through their fundamental belief system and provide the experience, if you will, of human connection and involvement.

The long and short of sustainable fundraising is about creating experiences for donors that they simply cannot obtain anywhere else. *The Eight Principles of Sustainable Fundraising* provides the framework and methods to help anyone in any fundraising capacity understand, reach and keep these individual investors as both current and long-term donors.

## The Coeur d'Alene Center for the Arts: A Case Study

In examining and applying the Eight Principles of Sustainable Fundraising™, we will look at a fictional nonprofit organization: the Coeur d'Alene Center for the Arts. Following each of the principles, the narrative of the Center for the Arts continues; these installments form a linear storyline, beginning with Principle 1: Donors are the Drivers.

This case study is developed using realistic situations within a fictional framework and will assist in looking at the real-life application of the principles discussed throughout this book. And while there is no specific organization on which the Center for the Arts is patterned, the situations presented are typical of many organizations—you may even see qualities of your own nonprofit in some of the following scenarios. Any similarities you may see to a specific nonprofit organization are purely coincidental.

This fictional organization is dedicated to the fine and performing arts and is located in the very real community of Coeur d'Alene, Idaho. Coeur d'Alene is a rapidly growing community in the Northern Panhandle of Idaho, and it is located about a half-hour drive east of Spokane, Washington. The area is home to over 40,000 residents and is the recreation, retail, manufacturing, healthcare, media and educational center of northern Idaho, also attracting a number of small businesspeople and artists to the area.

The Coeur d'Alene Center for the Arts, also known as CACA, was founded and incorporated in Idaho with a 501(c)(3) charter in 1981; its mission is to provide experiences in both the performing and fine arts to all citizens of Idaho's Northern Panhandle, with its services and activities concentrated in the community of Coeur d'Alene. "Making art accessible" is the CACA's unofficial motto.

The center provides a wide range of services, including art instruction to area school children, adult fine art instruction, juried shows featuring local artists, traveling art exhibits, lectures on a wide range of topics in the humanities, local musical and dance groups and traveling productions of newer Broadway fare. The CACA is a widely respected organization that has a favorable impact upon many groups within the area it serves; it also has a positive impact on the local economy.

The CACA has an annual operating budget of $2.5 million. Its primary revenue sources are: a membership program (10 percent); two long-time transactional fundraising events: the summer "Art Extravaganza," held in July, and a gala, held every October (50 percent); a small but stable group of individual donors (25 percent); and a few ongoing, relatively dependable grants from independent foundations (15 percent). The center's fiscal year runs from August 1 through July 31 of each year.

The board of the Center for the Arts is comprised of 17 individuals devoted to the arts, a number of whom have served for over 10 years. Although more focus has been placed upon the primary board activities of policy, advocacy and fundraising in recent years, the board still enjoys being "hands-on." Many members actively work with the school and adult programs, as well as participate in the art shows by submitting their own work.

With the growth of the operating budget to a comfortable level, the professional staff has grown in number and skill level. The executive director, Jane, leads and manages a staff of five including a program director, events coordinator and development officer. As already discussed, a program of individual giving, with an average gift size that is relatively modest but stable, contributes about one fourth of the center's revenue. In the last three or four years, however, the new donor acquisition program has been slowly decreasing. The only acquisition program is a spring mailing with names compiled from ticket sales and a purchased mass market list.

Now that we've explored the structure of the fictional Coeur d'Alene Center for the Arts, we can look at the principles in action. At the end of each chapter, you will see a "Currently at the Coeur d'Alene Center for the Arts" section, which will further explore the ideas discussed in the given principle.

# Principle 1

# Donors are the Drivers

"I would like a medium Vodka dry Martini—with a slice of lemon peel.  Shaken and not stirred, please."
— Ian Fleming, spoken by James Bond, *Casino Royale*

Donors *drive* philanthropy; they really do. Without them there is no philanthropy, no giving. It is, after all, their money. At the heart of every donor's decision to make a gift is the desire to actualize their personal values. Fundraisers who appreciate this and who seek to keep faith with both the donor and receiver perform an invaluable service for both the donor and the organization or cause they represent. Principle 1: Donors are the Drivers is the foundational principle for all sustainable philanthropy. This is the starting point for all lasting, successful fundraising efforts.

## Why are donors' values important?

We often think of donors as some alien class of beings who do not share the same desires, successes, failures, strengths and foibles common to humanity. We, perhaps, would never verbalize

**When we come to terms with the fact that donors are people just like us—and act upon this certainty—we have made the single most important step toward being successful in fundraising.**

such an assessment, but our actions betray us. By bringing our own values and assumptions to the table, we are not looking through the eyes of the prospective donor, but rather gazing through our own personal and/or organizational lens. When we come to terms with the fact that donors are people just like us—and act upon this certainty—we have made the single most important step toward being successful in fundraising.

We all have our own set of assumptions about life, which form our view of the world. The values we bring—those principles and precepts we hold dear—are the filter through which we *evaluate* people and circumstances. And so it is with donors. Central to these values is how we view money. Is it a tool to sustain our families and ourselves? Is it a giant piggy bank to satisfy our wishes and desires? Is it, in the right hands, a force for bringing about good? It is to this last view of money that philanthropists and would-be philanthropists subscribe. I add "would-be" inasmuch as the desire for participation in something greater than one's self is generally universal. Some philanthropists simply haven't identified themselves as such, yet.

But, what is the "good" donors want to support? Herein lies the crux of the concern for charities and nonprofits seeking to enlist the support (and funds) of philanthropists. In this case, the "good" is determined by the donor, who makes that determination through the lens of his or her values. When an organization asks for the financial support of potential donors using the organization's values, it has made the classic mistake in assuming either (1) the stated value is an unquestioned universal good, or—worse—(2) the donors have no preferences or proclivities other than the ones the organization espouses.

It's not merely those organizations who conduct business "on a shoestring" that, through their sense of urgency for funds, view their prospective supporters through this myopic lens. A few years back, I had the privilege to serve as campaign counsel for a well-established organization, which was conducting a capital campaign to erect a new home with truly first-rate facilities. When the case for support was submitted to me for review, I came across one line item in the "needs list" that leapt off the page. One of the "needs" for the campaign was for the provision of expansive and state-of-the-art staff offices. Their reasoning was that such an addition would justify the retention of a nationally renowned architect for the project.

Needless to say, lavish staff offices aren't the sorts of things that warm prospective donors' hearts. When I pointed this fact out to the client, there was no immediate recognition of the need to remove this glaring item; so inwardly focused were the senior team members of this organization that they were unable to see their faux pas. Ultimately, recognition set in, a change was made and the campaign went forward rather positively.

When one approaches fundraising from the charity's point of view, the result is predictable. Organizations send their message far and wide, while potential donors are—for the most part—hearing but barely listening. Imagine, if you will, an approach to potential donors that listens before speaking and asks before seeking to convince, and you will have begun the journey down the road to lasting fundraising success.

### Practice Point

*Identify the values and assumptions you make as a donor. What are they?*

*Consider all of the charitable organizations you currently support. Can you identify the values of each of those organizations that are aligned with your own?*

### What is philanthropy ultimately about?

Philanthropy is about giving *and* receiving. It's about reaching out to others and, at the same time, realizing your own dreams and goals. The Greek roots of the word, "philio" and "anthropos" suggest that the definition could literally be "for the love of mankind." As poetic as this is, it doesn't fully describe *what* philanthropy is, let alone *why* anyone does it.

Philanthropy is an activity that affects both the giver and receiver. Too often, we think of philanthropy as unilateral. In this view, the philanthropist gives to the worthy charity or nonprofit, and then the organization uses the gift to deliver their particular mission or agenda through programs that help others. This linear view of philanthropy finds its fullest manifestation in transactional fundraising—activities and events that obtain gifts through the sale or transfer of goods or services.

**Donors want to be *engaged*, not *enticed*.**

I, along with the chief executive of an organization I was serving, visited a businessman as a follow-up to an earlier meeting we'd had with him. The chief executive and I were engaging this individual, who had considerable personal wealth, in an attempt to discern the level and extent of his interest in the organization we were representing. My boss, the nonprofit chief executive, clearly felt a bit intimidated by the upfront, hard-charging style of the entrepreneur sitting opposite him. As with so many nonprofit leaders, my boss was focused on the potential level of funding. The businessman, on the other hand, was honing in on the expansiveness of the potential outcomes of an investment. The nonprofit executive was thinking of a transaction; the businessman was concerned with making an investment. Two ships passing in the night.

Donors want to be *engaged,* not *enticed.* In the former, the relationship between donor and organization is bilateral and reciprocally beneficial. There is the recognition that the fulfillment of donors' dreams and aspirations are as important as the fundraising goals. In the words of Stephen Covey, it's a "win-win."[3] When donors are engaged, they are invited inside, to become a part of something bigger than themselves. Moreover, they're invited in such a manner as is meaningful to *them*—the classic "pull" approach to involvement. When donors are "enticed," it's a one-way proposition with programs or needs being "pushed" at the donors—or worse—donors not really being asked for a gift at all, but rather sold a donated good or service in a transaction.

---

[3] Covey, Stephen R. *The 7 Habits of Highly Effective People.* Simon and Schuster, 1989.

The charity auction and golfing tournament, even children's baked goods and candy sales, rely upon this view of giving. You give, we use. This view of philanthropy holds that giving is about enticing donors, rather than engaging them. In doing so, it fails to take into account the fundamental motivations of donors, which are based on deeply held values and intangible benefits donors receive as a result of their giving. If the nonprofit executive had understood this, he would have been able to connect with the entrepreneur and, hopefully, create a long-term donor relationship.

At one point, I asked a reporter, who covers community and charity events for a recognized city daily newspaper, to conduct a little test. I asked her to take an informal survey of attendees at an upcoming, notable charity gala. At my request, she queried a dozen or so couples and individuals as to the reason for their attendance. After the event, I met with the reporter, who expressed astonishment at the responses she received. Not one of the attendees she polled as to their reasons for attendance was present for anything that remotely resembled a philanthropic or charitable motive. Reasons she heard ran the gamut from "my boss told me to help fill the corporate table" to "this is a great place to network" to "this event helps you stay on the social 'A' list." Some of those she surveyed didn't even know which charity was being benefited.

The bad news about such events is two-fold. First, you do not reach the audience that, by their interests and values, would best support you with direct giving. Secondly, you're not developing a renewable base of supporters, and, by the nature of such events with their "price sensitivity," you're ignoring and walking away from most of the true giving potential represented by those attending.

A better model of philanthropy would have benefactors and recipients being partners, while the charity serves simply as a broker to satisfy the needs of both. Here, the aphorism, "organizations don't have needs; people have needs," truly fits.

### Practice Point

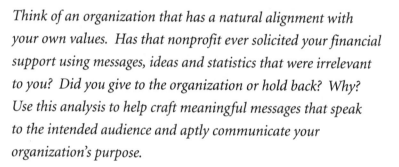

*As a* donor, *have you ever felt that "it is more blessed to give than to receive"? If so, did the recipient organization understand and appreciate your desire to engage in the organization's mission, or did they try to "sell" you their programs instead?*

*Think of an organization that has a natural alignment with your own values. Has that nonprofit ever solicited your financial support using messages, ideas and statistics that were irrelevant to you? Did you give to the organization or hold back? Why? Use this analysis to help craft meaningful messages that speak to the intended audience and aptly communicate your organization's purpose.*

### How can an organization engage donors?

So, how does an organization "engage" potential donors effectively? Most charities do this, if at all, through trial and error. Support is solicited using a message developed by the charity and guided by the charity's internal organization compass. Donors respond. This approach does work, as witnessed by the millions of donors and billions of dollars given each year to philanthropy in the United States.

Although this approach is very common among nonprofit organizations, it is only marginally effective. Many, if not the majority of, individuals who would potentially support the charity or worthy cause simply never hear or understand. Why? The message is sent but never received. It is either unintelligible to the receiver or simply ignored.

**Engaging people by first learning who they are and what is important to them allows a charity to fashion messages that will be understood, acted upon and appreciated.**

A charitable organization that seeks first to learn about its potential donors before attempting to enlist their support has, at once, sharpened its focus on those who are most likely to find kinship with the organization and, at the same time, significantly enlarges the financial potential from that group of would-be supporters. Learning about your potential donors is the first step. As such, it raises the *likelihood* of capacity levels of giving.

When I use the term "capacity," I am referring to a level of giving that is what the prospective donor *could* contribute if they were properly motivated to do so. Unfortunately, a great deal of giving is a calculated response to the unspoken question, "How little can I give and still keep my self-respect?" I refer to such giving as the "hush and go away gift"— considerably below what I could do but large enough so that I won't be bothered again (hopefully).

Engaging people by first learning who they are and what is important to them allows a charity to fashion messages that will be understood, acted upon and appreciated. The resulting effort is focused upon fewer people with greater (and potentially more lasting) results. After trying for weeks to get an appointment with an individual who had a long-time relationship with the organization I represented, I finally got my chance. Allen (not his real name) was a recently retired corporate executive who, through his recent departure from his company, had a "cash problem"— a high level of asset liquidity in a given tax year, which opened him to heavy taxation. Although anxious to reduce his tax exposure, he was very leery of any "do-gooder" who came seeking gifts; such was the case with me.

When I arrived to the meeting, he received me cordially but was nevertheless cautious. He explained that he had a team of accountants and tax attorneys working to "solve" his problem. I startled him when I asked him what *he* wanted to accomplish—what lasting legacy he would like to have. No one had ever asked him this question. Abruptly, he ceased talking of accountants and attorneys and became quite pensive. After a while, he told me that he and his wife cared for an adult daughter with severe mental disabilities. He wanted to somehow use his resources to aid other parents in similar situations as he knew of their anguish first-hand. Needless to say, I was taken a bit aback as Allen definitely fit the profile of being a genuine curmudgeon. What really caught me by surprise, however, was when I learned that, despite his twenty-five year history with this nonprofit organization in a leadership volunteer capacity, no one—from the executive on down—knew of his personal situation.

By asking a few thoughtful questions and listening without a prescribed agenda, I opened a totally new—and unexpected—reciprocally beneficial channel for both Allen and the nonprofit organization.

## *Practice Point*

*Identify five questions to ask your donors that might uncover what they want to accomplish in their giving.*

*How can your organization make changes to its outreach to donors, based on this new and enhanced understanding?*

## What do donors want?

Before volunteers or fundraisers can know or appreciate what donors *want*, they must first understand who donors *are*. Fundraisers often characterize donors as benevolent and generous…perhaps even "big hearted." Essentially, they're seen as community players who are merely "giving back" out of their excess, without much discrimination as to which charity their cash goes to. Fundraisers often operate from the perspective, either subconciously or deliberately, that giving is not really about giving, but exchanging. They believe there has to be some sort of material exchange or *quid pro quo* when a gift is made. This perspective leads to the transactional fundraising trap of high volume, high costs, low returns and low renewability. Fundraisers and volunteers alike tend to think that donors must be *enticed* to give through some sort of outsized recognition or identifiable "payback." This sort of thing appeals to very few donors, on the whole.

Penelope Burk's groundbreaking donor research explains that donors ultimately want just three things:[4]

1. Donors want to be acknowledged and thanked for their gifts.
2. Donors want to know that their gift was applied as they intended.
3. Donors want to know that their gift is achieving the desired outcome.

As a young major gifts officer, I had an experience that powerfully impacted me. I learned, through this experience, that donors are people first, with their own needs and aspirations; these needs must be addressed directly or indirectly in the gift-getting process. Over a period of some months, I met with a man who, in his role as the cofounder of a well-known technology firm, had acquired considerable wealth. An older

---

[4] Burk, Penelope. *Donor Centered Fundraising.* Cygnus Applied Research, 2003. 31.

gentleman (70+), he spent a good bit of his time working with a local venture capital group, looking for promising new start-ups. This man was capable and inclined to make a seven-figure gift to the organization I represented as he was seriously committed to its mission.

> **First and foremost, donors want to be seen for what they are—*investors.***

During one of our meetings, he confided in me that he had a serious reservation about making such a gift. As I listened carefully, I was running through my head for possible concerns he might have; I felt prepared to counter any reservations he had about the organization. What I heard astonished me. He said, "If I give you a serious gift, Larry, I'm afraid you won't come back to see me." For donors—investors—it's not about the money. It's about the relationship and the outcome.

First and foremost, donors want to be seen for what they are—investors. Investors are partners, peers. Investors want information about how a company is using their investment through products and services. Donors want information on the use and outcomes achieved by the charity with their investment. Investors want to be kept fully informed about where the company is and where it is going—before it becomes "yesterday's news." Donors want broader information about the organization and the context in which it operates. Investors want to be remembered…and thanked. So, too, donors want to be appreciated. Never forget that donors are first and foremost, people. Appearing on a list of donors is, in almost all cases, not nearly as important to a donor as being shown how his or her gift has been of critical value and made another's life worth living.

The idea that donors want and need to be thanked is one of those "obvious truths" that, by its very commonality, is often overlooked or given short shrift. How do you thank donors? In a manner that is meaningful to *them*. As chief advancement officer for a recognized institution, I had the privilege and honor of negotiating and closing an eight-figure gift, the largest to have ever been received by that institution. The donor couple, who I'll refer to as Bob and Liz, was modest, unassuming and wished to be definitely "low-key." Although certainly the largest and most organizationally significant, this was not their first gift to the institution as they had a history of giving modestly over several decades. About three weeks after the presentation of the proposal, Bob phoned me and simply said, "Liz and I have decided to do this. We're pleased to move forward." After expressing sincere thanks and placing the telephone back in its cradle, I let the words I had just heard sink in.

I immediately informed my boss, Carl, the organization's chief executive. "Ecstatic" may be the best word to describe Carl's reaction. Immediately, he assembled other senior players in the organization to discuss appropriate recognition. During the meeting, several "brass band" scenarios were bandied about. I urged restraint and caution, but told Carl that since Bob had phoned me, he should certainly place a call to Bob and Liz to offer his personal thanks. About a week later, I was traveling with Carl to visit other donors. As I drove the rental car away from the Atlanta Hartsfield Airport, I offhandedly asked Carl what Bob's and Liz's reactions were when he phoned them to say "thanks." He responded that he hadn't yet made the call. Horrified, I immediately moved out of six lanes of traffic to pull over and offer Carl my phone to call Bob and Liz immediately.

Here we had a well-meaning executive and institutional staff that were so focused on what they wanted to do to thank this couple that offering even the most direct, simple and personal appreciation of saying "thank you" was lost. Aside from saying "thank you," I often ask donors what sort of recognition, if any, they would find meaningful. By letter, by phone, by "opt-out" strategy, tailoring your appreciation is easy to do with even the most modest donors.

Donors *do* want appreciation. This is different from recognition, as we'll see later. They are also keenly focused on their gifts as *investments*. Donors (investors) want their gifts (investments) to be used by an organization that seeks to meet the needs of the community it serves within the context and bounds of their values. They want an organization that is prudent and effective. During the solicitation process, I learned that Bob and Liz, although long-time, modest donors, were only considering something truly transformational because the organization had made recent, substantial strides to professionalize its financial operations. Charities often sell themselves short, and even create a fundraising obstacle for themselves, when they only stress their low cost and minimal infrastructure. Beyond a reasonable point, donors are smart enough to know that cost that is "too low" is a short-term strategy.

Ann Goggins Gregory and Don Howard spoke eloquently to the need for adequate infrastructure—fundraising and otherwise—in their paper, *The Nonprofit Starvation Cycle*, published in the 2009 *Stanford Social Innovation Review* of the Stanford Graduate School of Business. By neglecting organizational infrastructure and stressing costs rather than effectiveness or outcomes, donors are given unrealistic expectations which in turn generate more pressure to conform. Nonprofit watchdog organizations, such as Charity Navigator and GuideStar, add to this conundrum by stressing cost factors in their ratings of charitable organizations. The irony of this situation is that donors, if given the opportunity, are far more interested in outcomes than costs—effectiveness over efficiency.

> **Charities who think in small terms end up getting what they ask for, which is very little.**

Donors want the charities they support to *thrive* and *succeed*, not merely "get by." A nonprofit organization that stresses mere survival has the unintended effect of communicating that investments there will have only minimal returns. Donors want to identify with a vision— a challenge bigger than they are, perhaps even bigger than life. Almost always unspoken is a donor's drive for a legacy, immortality. Charities who think in small terms end up getting what they ask for, which is very little. Such is the fate of those organizations driven by "cost" that they overlook true transformational opportunity.

### Practice Point

*On a piece of paper, list five examples of how your organization has treated donors as investors. Then, identify an area where your organization fits the "starvation" model. Use this list to evaluate what your organization is doing right—and what it could be doing better.*

### What is the difference between program focus and donor focus?

Nonprofits exist to fulfill a need in the community or communities they serve. That need can run the full gamut from enriching lives with art and music to providing the most basic necessities of life through food and shelter. Moreover, charitable organizations add value to their community in a larger, less tangible sense. The effectiveness of the nonprofit or charitable organization in fulfilling its mission is, quite understandably, of primary concern to staff and organizational leadership, as well as the individuals who are the recipients of the organization's efforts.

In seeking philanthropic donations, nonprofit organizations often conduct their fundraising efforts by promoting their *programming* to poten-

**People give to people.**

tial investors. A particular nonprofit may even seek to demonstrate the effectiveness and/or efficiency—that is, less cost for effort—of its programs. By doing so, the organization hopes to appeal to those who would potentially support the organization through their gifts. This approach to fundraising does raise money. It will not, however, even begin to approach the true giving capacity of an organization's donor constituency, nor will it engage investors in a manner that is sustainable and reasonably predictable over time.

For a charitable organization to achieve fundraising success that is both commensurate to its donor constituency's giving capacity and sustainable at the highest level over time, it must adopt a donor, rather than program, focus. Yes, programs are essential; they must be effective and relevant to the organization's mission. They should be designed and delivered, though, in a manner that is conditioned by the values and aims of their potential investors (i.e., donors).

People give to people. We've all heard this at some point. And, yet, how many of us actually take this statement at its most radical simplicity? Individuals make charitable gifts to enrich the lives and meet the needs of their fellow human beings. "Programming" is merely the vehicle—the conduit, if you will—and nothing more. The difficulty here is that the staff and leadership of nonprofits are far too often emotionally invested in a particular program or approach to fulfilling the charity's mission. In this scenario, it's easier to sell a program than solicit to ameliorate a need.

Donors have their own ideas about the needs of others and how to meet those needs. When they give, they are contributing within the framework of their personal values and, at the same time, seeking to realize those values. By "selling" a program, the charity at once separates the donor from the actual need; in doing so, it fails to acknowledge and act upon the values and aspirations of that particular donor.

A "donor focus" within an organization creates an organizational culture that seeks to identify and match the values of its potential investors to the needs of those it serves. In other words, it's not about the programming. The better the match, the closer an organization comes to truly commensurate giving—giving that represents donors' true financial capacities. Moreover, a good match increases the rate of donor renewability and, thus, fundraising program sustainability.

But, you may be thinking, we need to have programs to fulfill our mission. Exactly. In a donor-focused paradigm, however, investors drive the programs, not the other way around. This is a subtle, but essential, distinction.

### Practice Point

*Don't know what brings true satisfaction to your donors? Ask them. The best and most efficient way to obtain solid data on the goals and needs of your donors is to conduct a development program audit or assessment using a qualified consultant. You can also help to institute a culture of "continual feedback" and donor focus by carefully crafted donor surveys and selected personal contact.*
*In short, listen to people. They will tell you what they want. As they explain their values and concerns, listen for points of congruence with your organization's values.*

*An organization's board can be of great benefit by assigning
donors for individual board members to contact, simply to
inquire as to why the investor supports the organization.
But don't try to "piggy-back" such efforts with a solicitation
to "cut costs." Donors are people first and investors second—
they want to see that the organization is helping others in
the best way, not the cheapest way.*

## Currently at the Coeur d'Alene Center for the Arts

It's early August, and work on the upcoming fall annual giving campaign is in full swing. The current year operating budget was developed and approved at the board meeting in June. This year's Art Extravaganza, the summer art auction held every July, was predicted to produce a modest income growth of 5 percent. It didn't. With the soft economy, net revenues were actually down almost 10 percent from the previous year. Given that the event's revenue is counted in the fourth quarter of the fiscal year in which it occurs, it was pure luck that program expenses were unexpectedly light, thereby preventing a budget revenue deficit.

What happened? The Art Extravaganza has always been the big money generator for the center—the predictable over-the-top, hole-in-one resource that always produced. Although the available facts and figures concerning the event's performance in past years are of an accounting nature and not predictive, the board and the executive director, Jane, should have seen it coming. A closer look at the numbers would have shown that the revenue earned at the center's transactional fundraising events occurred during an economic period of "flush" money. This past year, though, event after event held in the Coeur d'Alene region fell short of both goals and expectations, bringing in less money than in years past.

The reality is that the center has been counting on revenue from responders, rather than donors. With little or no real relationship to the center, many of those who supported the auction in the past, and perhaps even attended it as a social occasion, simply decided to stay away this year. Others may have simply saw it as an art fair and exhibit with a modest gate fee of $10.

With Jane preparing for September's board meeting, she is openly re-evaluating the annual fundraising plan, which was approved only a couple of months ago. She's been wanting to move the center away from its heavy dependence on transactional fundraising, but has met with resistance in the past. Board members have seen healthy increases in these transactional sources for several years and have become quite emotionally attached to the social nature of the center's two major events, making them reluctant to comply.

Jane has asked Lauren, the center's development director, to come up with a fundraising plan that begins the shift toward a more robust individual giving program. Handling the revenue shift will be tricky—they're both in uncharted territory, and they know it. Not only are they unaware of the immediate revenue impact such a shift will bring—positive or negative—they really don't know very much about the CACA's current individual donors. Well, yes, they know their addresses and giving histories; basic record keeping is sound. What they don't know is why these donors give from year to year. Moreover, they don't know why average gift size has remained remarkably consistent from year to year—neither up nor down. Even more troubling is a slight but noticeable trend downward, in recent years, in the percentage of new donors that are minted each year from the new names of prospects that come in through referral, membership, and the general profile mass mailing list that is purchased each year from an outside vendor.

Lauren instinctively knows that, if the fundraising programs aimed at individual donors are to grow and impact the bottom line of the center, there needs to be some basic research conducted on donor values and interests. In the past, she's suggested that a consultant be brought in to conduct such research and provide this data, but she has been told consultants are expensive, and besides, donors need to be informed, first and foremost, of what the CACA needs.

Jane and Lauren have some difficult tasks ahead of them. First, they must sell a change in fundraising direction to a board that dearly loves its events and believes that simply working harder will achieve the needed additional revenue. Second, they must engage the board in becoming a part of the solution. Let's explore the ideas in Principle 1: Donors are the Drivers to help come up with some ideas for how they might address this dilemma.

## Questions to Consider

1. How is Principle 1: Donors are the Drivers impacting the center? Is the center donor-focused or program-focused?

2. How might Jane and Lauren begin to engage not only donors, but also board members?

3. How aggressive should the CACA be in changing the current program, and what level of risk should they be willing to incur?

4. What are the potential roadblocks to change in this situation, and can you identify a "work around" plan for each.

# Principle 2

# Begin at the Beginning

"Let's start at the very beginning, a very good place to start."
— Oscar Hammerstein II, sung by Maria, *The Sound of Music*

If the beginning point for all philanthropy is the donor, the next step is to identify how to effectively attract investors to an organization. But before a donor can be expected to invest serious resources into a cause, an organization must not only know what it wants to accomplish, but also how to frame that knowledge within the worldview and concerns of the donor. Principle 2: Begin at the Beginning demands that an organization does its due diligence in obtaining that self knowledge and then translating that into the perspective of the donor.

## What do I want to accomplish?

The answer to this seems obvious, doesn't it? I (or we) want to raise more money, develop new programs, enlarge existing ones and "help" more people. Really? Such could be said for practically every nonprofit organization in America. Organizations adopting such a general, almost generic, objective are very likely to achieve similarly vague, non-measurable results.

Other nonprofits begin their efforts with a clear idea of who they are, whom they serve and what they want to accomplish. Over time, the organization's mission becomes more diffuse, less definite or, perhaps, even set in a different direction altogether. "Mission creep," as it is sometimes called, saps away an organization's fundraising strength by confusing or alienating those who currently support it, while garnering only tepid attention of others. So, what's a nonprofit to do?

**Investors, donors who will support you through thick and thin, demand clarity.**

Your favorite charity may, indeed, want to raise more money and serve more people. There's nothing wrong there. To achieve this, however, requires a clarity of vision and specificity of

42

result that leaves absolutely no room for ambiguity. Be expansive, but be specific. Objectives should certainly have an element of "blue sky" but not be totally devoid of reality. Interestingly, clarity and specifics can make organizational

> **The more ambitious your vision, the more likely you are to attract the significant investors.**

leadership (boards, especially) a bit uncomfortable, even squeamish. The clearer the objectives, the clearer the responsibilities and requirements of all involved—that's where it can get sticky.

Investors, donors who will support you through thick and thin, demand clarity. They want a vision that is both expansive and grounded in reality. They want objectives that they can feel and touch—objectives that make sense to *them*. And it just so happens that the more specific and measurable your objectives are, the greater the probability that you will actually achieve them. The more ambitious your vision, the more likely you are to attract the significant investors who will be in a position to provide the resources to make that vision a reality.

Teach for America is a perfect example of a successful charity with a clear mission. Wendy Kopp, the CEO and founder, articulated a grand vision of a national teaching corps of young college graduates working in America's neediest schools. What began as nothing but a dream has resulted in over twelve thousand young adults having taught well over two million students since the organization's founding in 1990. Teach for America also raised $41 million dollars in 2005 to support their work, and the organization is still thriving today.

## *Practice Point*

*Want to get a fix on how "firm" the organization's
mission is, how broadly understood? Ask the body that
is charged with protecting that mission—the governing board.
At a board meeting, have each member of the board take a piece
of paper and write the mission statement; if you're bold enough,
go around the room and ask members to verbally quote the
mission statement. You know you have work to do when
board members—the keepers of the flame—have trouble
doing this correctly.*

*Is your organization's mission statement too long to easily
remember? That's a sure sign that it's probably too lengthy,
too convoluted or too detailed. Mission statements are clear,
concise statements of purpose, not policy lists.*

*Creating a mission statement that reflects the vision of your
organization is a subject that can occupy whole workshops.
For an effective but simple start, write answers to the following
questions on a piece of paper:*

- *Why this? Detail the need or cause your organization
  focuses on.*
- *Why us? Describe your organization's place in fulfilling
  the need.*
- *Why now? Explain the reasons for urgency or for simply
  not doing anything.*

*Remember, your answers need to be meaningful to your donors,
not just your organization. Use your answers to write a concise
mission statement that includes these three elements.*

**How can I accomplish my mission? How do I fund it?**

Now that you have a specific, concise mission statement and know what you want to achieve in order to make the world a better place, how will you go about achieving it? How will you fund it? At your very first planning meeting, fundraising needs to be addressed. Choosing the role fundraising activities will play in your organization is critical to success. Too

> **Investors trust your organization with more than their financial resources.**

often, organizations see fundraising as something that is conducted separate from the main purposes of the organization. The organizations that have the healthiest, most productive fundraising programs make fundraising an equal partner with delivering core programs and services. "It's simply who we are," is an oft-heard response. These donor-driven programs are never merely servants doing the bidding of self-directed programs. For potential investors (donors) the "what" is as, if not more, important than the "how." Being stepwise and cogent in your approach will give potential donors confidence that you know what you're doing and you're committed to doing it.

Investors trust your organization with more than their financial resources. In fact, they trust you with their values and higher life purpose. Giving is both rational and irrational, head and heart. A donor who is an *investor* is fully *vested*. Naturally, someone who is involved with, and attached to, the organization in this way is eager to hear of incremental progress—the organization's successes and its failures. Persons that have invested their hearts and minds into a project or organization can feel neglected or frustrated if they aren't kept "in the loop." As Spinoza stated, "Nature abhors a vacuum." If you don't provide timely, meaningful communication, donors will fill the space with misconceptions—or worse—some other charitable interest. Here again, the relative modifiers, "timely" and "meaningful," are determined by your investors…not by your organization.

Sharing details with potential investors will build the confidence level of those very individuals who will support your undertaking through both money and time. Don't be overly concerned that such specificity will "scare away" potential investors who don't agree with you. The reality is that if a potential donor chooses not to support you because of your position, perspective or approach to the issues at hand, you never really had their support, anyway. Being particular in your approach is quite effective in *defining* who will actually invest in your cause and become a part of your "donor constituency." No one will support everything. Being specific and unapologetic about what you are about will bring your supporters into focus, give them confidence in what your organization stands for and strengthen their commitment, both financial and otherwise.

### *Practice Point*

*Identify the primary value or higher purpose of your organization that you believe your donors share.*

*After you've identified this primary value, test it with a few, randomly chosen donors. Ask them what they think your primary value is. Do they agree?*

*Discovering your donors' values and interests, and then comparing how well they align with your organization's values, will quickly separate fact from assumption. Using an independent professional or research process is often the fastest and most objective way of doing so.*

## Why this? Why now? Why us?

These three questions are essential elements that an organization must continually communicate to all those who would potentially support it. In fundraising parlance, the answers to these questions comprise your "case for support." The term comes from the legal environment, where an advocate, your attorney, makes the argument for your position before a judge and jury. As in the legal sense, third parties will ultimately assess your organization and make their decisions of support accordingly—from *their* frame of reference.

But, what does each of the aforementioned questions mean? "Why this?" speaks to the need to distinguish your organization's goals and approaches from others and to make an argument for them. The answer will mostly likely not be self-evident among those who would potentially support you; here again, the specifics are essential. The answer to "Why now?" should communicate a sense of urgency and timeliness to potential donors for the issue you seek to support. "Sounds good, but I don't understand the push," is an oft-heard comment. "Why us?" is the question with the greatest potential impact upon an organization's fundraising. This is your organization's opportunity to distinguish itself from others, to shine above the rest, to offer the "only available here" donor experience. Your answer to this question will address your organization's effectiveness, its reputation and the clarity of its vision.

The most difficult part of answering these questions is not in having answers but in framing the answers within potential investors' worldview and perspective. Notice the singular of "worldview" and "perspective." Even among established organizations with professional development staffs, keeping investors' perspectives front-and-center isn't easy and requires constant diligence. I was once given a spring annual fund direct mail piece to review. This solicitation, from an established, mature nonprofit with a multi-million dollar operating budget, was to be mailed to all donors who had made gifts in previous years but not the current year (what fundraisers call SYBUNTS—some years but not this). As I read the letter, one sentence leapt off the page. "As our fiscal year moves into its final quarter," the sentence read, "your gift is critical to our ongoing programs. At this writing we need an additional $101,467.52 to balance our budget for the year and continue to operate." The number quoted was actually the figure used for an internally tracked, budgeted line item for fundraising. Rather than urging donors to participate in this year's annual drive, what was communicated to individuals who had supported the organization regularly in the past was a sense of panic, desperation and possible mismanagement. After reading this, I immediately phoned the fundraising committee chairperson and asked his reaction to the sentence after I read it to him. His response was, "The same reaction I had the first time I read it." What I thought was a draft was actually already on the street.

In this case, the motive—if not the effect—of the annual fund drive mailing was to encourage past donors to make a gift to support the current year's goal. Instead of the approach that was used, why not something like, "Your past support has been of great value to our (insert something mission specific), and I know (assumes an individual has actually signed the correspondence) that you will want to be counted as we are over 75% toward our goal of $500,000 to provide critical operating funds for (insert appropriate phrase)." Sound a little different? What was a message of desperation and mismanagement is now an invitation to renew a worthy investment.

### *Practice Point*

*Want to know how a message will be received before sending it? Ask. Here again, your investors—select ones in this case—will be quite pleased to be solicited for their honest, candid feedback. Test everything…and not just with those inside of the organization. Key board members can be of assistance here, but don't forget the "rank and file" who compose the bulk of your supporters. After asking for honest feedback, double your impact by following up with those you asked. In doing so, let them know how their responses will shape your future communication with them.*

### How does the medium shape the message?

Marshal McCullen's groundbreaking book, *Understanding Media* (1964), went so far as to postulate that how we communicate a message is the message itself. This is perhaps a hyperbole, but what we say is certainly shaped by the manner in which we say it and the channels of communication we use to deliver it. In face-to-face encounters, body language is a much larger component of communication than the words verbalized. From there on out, all methods of communication—phone calls, mail, email, mass media, social media—have their particular quirks and benefits. Communicating a message, then, *is* shaped by the channel or vehicle with which we choose to communicate. It may be the same message, but it sounds "different" depending upon how and to *whom* it is being communicated.

Why? Because, quite simply, receivers receive messages differently. This is not only because different people perceive things differently, but the manner in which it is communicated also shapes the actual content of what is received and interpreted. Board members, new donors, long-time supporters and competitors (yes, competitors) all need information. All of it should be consistent but presented in a way that will be properly understood by the particular receiver.

In this way, the channel or "medium" does shape the message being sent. More detail, less detail, choice of vocabulary, frequency of communication, timing of communication, emphasis on select areas—these are the variables of a shaped message. Think about both to whom the message is going and *how* and when it will be sent before you craft it. To individuals on the "outside" of the organization, their perceptions are developed through what they read, hear and see.

At an organization I was serving, we conducted a survey to determine exactly who was receiving what communications when. Since this was a large, multi-faceted organization, it wasn't simply the public relations and marketing departments that were communicating with the donors. We reached out across the organization to gather all of the data and created a month-to-month calendar that was cross-referenced by each of the major external constituent groups, including board members, advisory panel members, program attendees, major donors and annual giving donors, among others. We looked at all of the relevant channels of both personal and group communication such as personal visit, phone, email and postal service correspondence. What we discovered was that individuals were often receiving communication in great spurts, followed by periods of almost total silence. What's more, gift solicitations were actually being sent on top of each other. Due in part to the results of this survey, the organization did a total revamp of external communications. In the new system, all sources were integrated and sequenced so that donors received a cogent, respectful and meaningful (to them) flow of information.

## *Practice Point*

*Constructing a simple timeline communications grid, like the one described in the previous section, can reveal a lot about your organization's communication, or lack thereof. This can be especially beneficial in large organizations in which many departments are responsible for communicating with donors. It's almost a given that you'll see holes and clusters of communication efforts. Use this analysis to help smooth the flow of communication and achieve maximum impact with the least amount of duplication or redundancy.*

### Currently at the Coeur d'Alene Center for the Arts

The mission of the center has always been, more or less, "making art accessible." It's what has guided the CACA's founders, and the mission continues with those in leadership today. And although virtually everyone who is associated with the center—staff, volunteers, board members, program participants, informed community members—could repeat this simple statement of purpose, very few could tell you precisely what it means or what the ultimate impact of the center in the community really is. If you ask someone what this means, you will most likely get an answer that is relevant to the responder. That's not necessarily bad; it's reality. The difficulty is that both staff and board members at the center assume their individual interpretation of the mission is the operative one. As long as enrollment or attendance at the various programs and events remains healthy, neither staff nor board members question this wisdom.

Jane, the executive director, really wants an all-out reevaluation of the center's programs, from top to bottom. David, the program director, is mildly supportive; but like many with a "program" focus, he is inherently suspicious of those on the outside, such as donors, influencing what happens on the inside. Lauren, the development director, wants to create a program for collecting and understanding donor feedback. But she's a bit stymied as to where to begin, as she has limited resources; furthermore, she is not convinced that Jane is all that in favor of taking donor interests seriously.

The revised fundraising plan that Lauren and Jane are now working on has to be incorporated into the revised operating plan; this new plan will be reviewed at the upcoming September board meeting. A meeting has been scheduled with Jane, Lauren and David, with the primary objective to get David to become an active supporter of the need to learn donor interests...or at least not be a naysayer. Lauren is also interested in "testing" Jane's commitment to moving away from the center's reliance on transactional fundraising. Lauren knows it's one thing to say you want a new approach, when what you really want are the results of a different program—not the change necessary to implement it. Lauren needs to sort out her options and come prepared to be persuasive in her plans to move the center's fundraising efforts forward. Let's examine how Principle 2: Begin at the Beginning can help Lauren communicate her concerns and ideas with Jane and David, while convincing them to take a donor-focused approach.

## Questions to Consider

1. How is Principle 2: Begin at the Beginning impacting the operations and future of the center?

2. Given the limited information, what facts might the board want to know before finalizing the fundraising plan?

3. What's at stake here with regard to donor interests and preferences, and how might these elements affect the content and delivery of future programs?

4. Can you think of any potential difficulties in implementing the new plan? If so, what are they?

5. How would such change be accepted in your own organization? What will be the likely trouble spots?

# Principle 3

# Leadership Leads

"Eighty percent of success is showing up."
— Woody Allen

Hardly anyone would question the concept of leadership by example. And yet, many fall victim to the idea that leadership is somehow "do as I say, not as I do." But building a fundraising program that delivers a renewable, repeatable stream of philanthropic revenue demands the loyalty and trust of those investing. We earn that trust through our actions and, more specifically, how close our actions correspond to our words. Principle 3: Leadership Leads is perhaps the most powerful tool in reducing fundraising anxiety. When a leader sets the example, he or she can move with confidence; even if others decide not to follow the example, respect is earned for another day or time.

### Why does the board have to go first?

People expect leaders to *lead.* So it is with charitable organizations. Board members, collectively and individually, ARE the leadership of the organization. It is the board, not the executive staff, which ultimately determines the future direction and health of a nonprofit organization. The board sets the overall direction and the staff implements it. The responsibilities of the board can really be distilled down to three fundamental activities:

1. The board, collectively and individually, must continually advocate the organization to the community and the constituencies from which it hopes to receive revenue.

2. The board must set the policy for the organization.

3. Board members must be actively involved in the fundraising process.

That's it.

Many times, boards would rather involve themselves in the operations of the organization rather than in advocacy, fundraising or policy. If this is the comfort zone of some of your board members, you probably need to consider inviting these individuals to serve in an area where operations need help—and not on the board. Operations are the purview of the executive director or chief staff member. Staff members need the boundaries set by organizational policy, the favorable climate established by advocacy and the revenue generated by active fundraising to perform effectively. The sum total of board involvement could be termed "strategic support." Without such support, operations are without long-term direction and often flounder.

With this in mind, the term "going first" usually refers to the board's involvement in fundraising. In philanthropic, as in most other endeavors, potential donors respond in kind to the tone and character of the example of leadership—in this case, that is the board. Board members need to set both the example and pace for larger giving, and current and potential donors will gauge their own responses to the performance of the board. There is the old adage that anyone with authority to spend money must also have the responsibility to raise it. Such is essential with nonprofit boards.

"But, our board is representative of our community and does not have many members with 'deep pockets,'" you may be thinking. The key to effective board fundraising performance is *commensurate giving*, that is, giving by each member commensurate to his or her financial ability. Like the larger donor pool, the board is not uniform in its giving ability across membership. Therefore, a well-performing board, from a fundraising sense, occurs when each member is actively and regularly making gifts that are commensurate with each member's true giving capacity. When a board is giving to this capacity, several things happen. First, the level of each member's commitment to the organization rises.

Second, confidence among members as to the ability of the organization to achieve fundraising success rises. Third, and perhaps most important, healthy giving by the board sends the clearest, most positive signal to potential donors that this organization is a good place to invest.

## *Practice Point*

*Name two things in each of the three areas of board responsibility (advocacy, policy and fundraising) that your organization's board does well. Next, consider if the board strays outside of the three fundamental responsibilities.*

*If you are having trouble thinking of examples for any of the areas of responsibility, think of three ideas for how the board's energy could be used more productively.*

### What sort of commitment to the organization does the board need to have?

The aphorism "time, talent and treasure" applies here. You'll often hear that, since Jessica is so liberal with her commitment of time, a financial gift shouldn't be expected. Jim may be on the board for "big gifts" but isn't expected to contribute his talent to the leadership of the organization. Board commitment is not *either/or*—it is *both/and*. In this case, it is all three: without a commitment of time, the contribution of talent and the sacrifice of a financial gift, a board member's engagement will lack the critical mass to move the organization forward.

Regrettably, board membership in some nonprofits is treated as a perk or reward for other service to the organization. Rather, board membership is a very particular volunteer assignment with specific duties and responsibilities. If individuals are unable or unwilling to assume those responsibilities, there are plenty of other volunteer opportunities where their skill, talent and expertise will be invaluable.

Board members are also sometimes recruited for their "name," rather than their commitment. Name alone will not engender commitment from others. Effective board membership is not about lending your name to an organization or collecting resume perks. It's about focusing your talents, energies and finances on an organization that engages both your mind and heart, while enhancing your passion for the mission. Effective board members are active, strategic catalysts for the organization, not dispassionate, passive caretakers.

Don't assume that by not expecting all board members to be donors, you will avoid the awkwardness of putting someone "on the spot." A social worker once approached me and shared her experience serving on a nonprofit's board. Linda (not her real name) had been on this organization's board for almost five years but had yet to be asked for a gift. As a member of an underrepresented minority in the community, she felt out of place at board meetings as she looked around the room and saw wealth and privilege sitting around the table. Since she had not been asked for a gift, she assumed that her gift— albeit a small one—would be of little or no value. As a consequence, she also felt reluctant to weigh in on board business. By the time she and I had our conversation, she had concluded—rightly or wrongly— that she was on the board as a "token," a window dressing for the organization's public relations.

What a tragedy. Here was an individual who wanted to give and participate but didn't feel valued enough to do so. All gifts have value. The key to being a part of the team is commensurate giving; equal sacrifice, not equal dollars. No board member should be exempt.

## Practice Point

*If you are a board member, a simple test is to ask yourself if the organization you serve is among the top three that you support with your own gifts. Does this organization garner your top-tier support?*

*Do your current financial contributions reflect your commitment to the organization?*

*If the organization you serve is not in the top three, consider adjusting your current giving level or finding another way to serve the organization.*

### What is the strategic construction of a board?

Much of what constitutes sustainable fundraising results from careful planning and deliberate decisions based upon end objectives. The board, as the single most important volunteer group in any organization's fundraising, should be comprised of individuals who have been chosen deliberately and specifically. Too often, nonprofit organizations use board membership as a reward for devoted or exemplary volunteer service. Such an appointment does both the individual and organization a significant disservice. Board membership is not a reward; it is a responsibility. It is not, as some think, necessarily the highest, most prestigious volunteer post. It is a very specific volunteer post with a specific set of requirements and responsibilities, and it isn't for everyone. In other arenas, companies have made the mistake of promoting their most

**Too often, nonprofit organizations use board membership as a reward for devoted or exemplary volunteer service.**

creative talent into line management positions as a reward. The result is often a frustrated individual, robbed of what he or she does best and giving mediocre performance. Nonprofit board membership is no different.

> **The ability to speak for, and relate to, the various giving constituencies is an essential quality of board membership.**

A strategically constructed board consists of two main elements. First, membership should be chosen so that all significant donor constituencies are represented. The ability to speak for, and relate to, the various giving constituencies is an essential quality of board membership. Board members must also be integrally involved in the fundraising process. As we will see in Principle 7: Renew & Refresh, board members serve as invaluable resources by using their personal and professional networks to identify potential donors. Accessing these networks is one of the most important board responsibilities, with respect to fundraising, because it serves not only the effort to identify prospective donors, but also its precursor—general advocacy.

There are certainly other considerations in assembling the right individuals to come together into a well-rounded and effective board, but the two main areas—donor constituency representation and advocacy—must be met. If these requirements aren't fulfilled, the board and subsequently the organization will struggle.

### *Practice Point*

*Nonprofit boards that function well and work as cohesive units don't come together by themselves. Rather, they are the result of careful planning and rigorous, ongoing evaluation. You can go a long way to getting your organization's board focused by having the board conduct an annual evaluation of themselves as a group, as well as evaluating each individual board member.*

*Board evaluations can be conducted using carefully constructed, blindly evaluated, written questionnaires which seek to identify both strengths and weaknesses. Nonprofit governance organizations can provide templates of evaluation instruments at nominal fees.*

*Board evaluations are also a part of a development program assessment or audit conducted by a qualified consultant. This approach is sometimes used to get a true third-party perspective. If your organization's board is new to an evaluation process for both the group and individual members, getting outside expertise is likely to yield far superior results than a self-initiated process, while incurring a lot less emotional pain.*

## What skills should I be looking for in a board member?

Although this is not a skill, an essential quality of all board members is a true belief in, and identification with, the mission of the organization. Without this, even the most polished and accomplished individual will be of little value to the organization. That being said, belief in the mission is necessary, but not sufficient. Having the heart for the work is critical, but not sufficient enough to be effective either. There are a myriad of skills that the board should collectively possess. Enlistment of board members should be executed with a clear knowledge of what is needed at any particular time.

The "typical" committee structure lends itself to thinking about skill sets. This is why we have a governance committee, finance committee, program committee, development or fundraising committee and, perhaps, a separate communications and public relations committee. Public relations is often combined with fundraising, as they are natural partners. We'll need board members with experience and ability moving groups of individuals forward, as well as board members that have accounting and/or financial acumen. Persons who have an interest and/or experience in the organization's programs will be needed. Individuals who have experience and/or interest in fundraising, as well as those who have an understanding of advocacy, are essential.

Recruitment should never be driven by the availability of a particular candidate, no matter how desirable. Candidates for any enlistment should be carefully screened and vetted so that their profiles and skill sets match the current needs of the organization. For example, "Mary may be excellent board member material, but we really don't need four accountants at this time. Perhaps later."

### *Practice Point*

*Think about your personal skills and strengths. Are they being used effectively for the organization(s) you currently serve? Are they being used at all?*

*Next, consider whether or not the leadership of the organization(s) you serve recognizes these skills and strengths. If not, consider approaching a board member or person in leadership to discuss how your skills might be best utilized.*

*You can also do a quick "skills survey" of the board by writing each member's name on a piece of paper. Next to each name, list the skills and talents you believe each person brings to the table. Then, use the list to assess whether those skills are being used effectively and whether they are complimenting or repeating the skills of others.*

**What does commitment really mean for a board member?**

Volunteers—even leadership volunteers such as board members—want to know what a "good job" looks like.

I've discussed that the components of commitment are time, talent and treasure. A position description that clearly delineates the nature of this commitment is essential in keeping faith with a volunteer, as well as enabling him or her to perform well. All volunteers—even leadership volunteers such as board members—want to know what a "good job" looks like. They want to know what is required of them. They want to know what "success" looks like—for them as well as for the organization. They want to know how much time it will take and what financial sacrifice will be necessary. Giving a board member or other volunteer a clear sense of the time commitment required is often of greater importance to the individual than even the financial requirement. Organizations who sidestep or soft-pedal the specifics during an enlistment do no one a favor.

There are several things that should be expected of a board member. As to time, certainly a minimum attendance at meetings should be defined and expected. Participation in committee deliberations and attendance at major fundraising and public relations functions is also in the mix. Time spent in individual activities, such as personal advocacy, potential donor referrals, donor cultivation and donor stewardship, round out the time element. Presumably, the organization is aware of the individual's talent, thus it should be expected that the particular skills they bring to the table will be engaged. Don't assume that, just because a potential board member is talented or skillful in a particular arena, he or she will be willing to engage that ability for the benefit of the organization. Ask. Finally, treasure, although a relative term, is the requirement that all board members can and must meet. Personal giving amounts need not be—and almost never are—equal. The financial sacrifice required, however, should be. Those already familiar with fundraising know that the Pareto Principle is operating. That is,

> **Don't assume that, just because a potential board member is talented or skillful in a particular arena, he or she will be willing to engage that ability for the benefit of the organization.**

about 80 percent or more of your gifts will come from about 20 percent or less of those giving. With respect to giving, a good rule of thumb is that the nonprofits for which board members serve should be in the top three to which they financially contribute.

## Practice Point

*Do your organization's board members understand their commitment needs to include time, talent and personal treasure? To take the "pulse" on commitment, construct a "commitment grid" using the variables of time, talent and treasure and cross list these with each board member's name. Then, evaluate each current board member against these qualities. You might use a scale of 1–5, with 5 being totally committed and 1 being "missing in action."*

*Now, evaluate the results. What's the average level for the entire board in each of the three qualities? Are you happy with what you see? Do any particular members of the board stand out—either as strong or weak? In fairness to the members of your*

*organization's board, research has shown that the vast majority of*
*nonprofits never give their board members clear expectations of*
*performance nor do they provide any training for these key leaders.*
*How can your organization change this trend?*

## How does the board fit into the larger portfolio of volunteers?

The board, quite simply, is the *leadership* group. They *lead*. It may sound simple, but this concept can often get lost in a "to do" list. The leadership that board members must be about is leadership by example. They must focus on the essence of their responsibilities in advocacy, fundraising and policy formation, while setting an obvious and public example. Such leadership is critical in the fundraising process. Without it, board members are only passengers in a boat with no oars, at best, and with anchors over the side, at worst.

By focusing on its particular responsibilities, the board actually enables and empowers other volunteers. When the board provides a receptive community environment through positive advocacy, volunteers are encouraged and motivated. When the board provides appropriate and stable funding, volunteers have the assurance that their efforts are worth the investment. When the board sets and maintains proper policy, volunteers sense the stability of the organization. Conversely, when the board's focus is off the essentials—advocacy, fundraising and policy—the organization is set adrift. In this scenario, volunteers are essentially "on their own" to accomplish what they can. Such is a prescription for a great deal of well-intentioned effort that often results in frustration and lack of accomplishment by the volunteers—and the staff.

## *Practice Point*

*Are some of your organization's board members currently "off task," focused on concerns outside of advocacy, policy and fundraising? If so, identify other possible places of service for those particular board members. Consider how to refocus their energies or redirect their enthusiasm to other places in the organization, other than board membership, that would be both rewarding to them and beneficial to the organization.*

### Currently at the Coeur d'Alene Center for the Arts

The board members of the center, all 17 of them, are devoted to the betterment of the center—as they see it. Almost half have served on the board for at least 10 years, and there are even a handful of the original founders of the center still serving. This group is very program oriented as they were a part of the cadre of individuals who not only had the original vision, but literally did everything before there was a single paid staff member. Old habits die hard, and this core group sees their role as protecting the original purpose of the center. Furthermore, they are not shy about offering their input on programming and operations down to the color of table linens at events.

The current board chair, Jack, is a local public accountant with his own firm; he also dabbles in funding business start-ups and is anxious to put the CACA on a more systematic and sound business footing. He's served on the board for only two years, but he is a bit impatient to "get things moving," as he puts it. Although well-meaning, he has virtually no experience with relational fundraising. Luckily, he uses the principles of permission market-ing in his own business ventures, so he is teachable.

Jack is all about cash and is very concerned about stabilizing and increasing the flow of it. He's not easily reassured by history, unlike many of his counterparts on the board with longer tenures, who easily dismissed this past summer's drop in auction revenues as a fluke. He sees all too well the effect of reduced consumer discretionary spending in the local economy, and he has openly wondered if ticket sales and enrollment fees are the next to suffer from the weak economy.

But there are some other issues in the fundraising process that the board isn't addressing. In regards to board giving, about 70 percent of the members do make some sort of gift annually from their own resources. The gifts are "passive," as they are not solicited, and the timing and amounts do not exhibit any pat-tern. As to participating in the fundraising process, less than a fourth of board members are actively involved in an activity that reinforces individual giving in any way. One individual writes the two renewing grants that the center receives each year, and an-other board member takes pride in having helped in asking a couple of community notables to contribute...once...five years ago. The rest of the board members serve in logistical capacities for the fundraising events.

Three board members, Sally, John, and Claire, have been on the board since the center's inception. They take it as a matter of personal pride that they are part of the "founding few" yet that seems to be where their interest stops. Except for Claire, they haven't attended a board meeting for over a year. Although none of the three make personal gifts, they are usually "front and center" at the Art Extravaganza, each summer. Jack has hinted to

Jane that there needs to be some reorganization of the board, perhaps beginning with this group, but to put it in her words, she simply doesn't "want to go there."

Jack wants to see "things happen" but he is a very busy man. When Jane says she wants change but seems reluctant to take real risks, he doesn't push it. After all, there is plenty to keep him busy at his firm. He has met Lauren in the past, but has not had much contact with her. Nonetheless, he senses she has energy and good ideas and would welcome more time to work with her.

In addition to some individuals lacking commitment, board members do not review the productivity of the CACA's fundraising programs. Since the organization has been steady in its fundraising in the past years, they have not seen much need to. Until the recent local economic downturn, the board saw little reason to evaluate their programs. But fundraising is not a special case. The board has never formally evaluated its performance with respect to any of its areas of responsibility, either individually or collectively.

Lauren knows that, to get the center's program of individual giving on a more aggressive footing, the board must have a more direct role in fundraising efforts—and take responsibility for the outcome. Now that the fiscal year is beginning anew, she believes now is the time to make some serious change, but she is a bit uncertain as to how to proceed. Let's look at how Principle 3: Leadership Leads, might help Lauren approach this task.

## Questions to Consider

1. How is Principle 3: Leadership Leads impacting the operations and future of the CACA?

2. How might Lauren build immediate support and commitment to fundraising within the board?

3. How can Jane, the executive director, move the board to a more systematic and aggressive fundraising posture? How might she build upon their preconceptions about their role as a board, as well as the organization's mission, to move the CACA to the next level?

4. In your view, what is the most serious impediment to getting the CACA board to take a more active role in fundraising—both internally and in supporting and participating in a program of true relational fundraising? How would you go about removing that impediment, or at least "neutralizing" it?

# Principle 4

# Learn & Plan

"Learn the lines and don't bump into the furniture."
— Noel Coward

Raising money that is renewable and sustainable is more like surgery than panning for gold, although there are elements of both in effective fundraising. Surgery requires specific knowledge and skill—of both the patient and the process. Panning for gold is the routine, laborious task of sifting through gravel for the nuggets. Principle 4: Learn & Plan, is the surgical procedure in fundraising. To be effective, your organization must know specifically who may have the inclination to support it's mission, and exhibit skill, through planning, to build a relationship with those potential donors.

**Before I plan, whom should I raise money from?**

There often isn't much thought given to the answer of this question, except for "anyone and everyone." Ask Jim, he has money. So does Sally. The irony is that, for your organization, the answer is already determined, even before the question is asked. Sustainable fundraising is driven by donors who are engaged in the mission of the organization. Therefore, a charity's mission has already determined who will give.

Defining your mission with clarity, conviction and attention to a potential donor's perspective becomes critical to the success of the organization's fundraising efforts, as it will ultimately define the donor pool. Prospective donor pools aren't determined by wealth or even proximity. They are decided by what the organization has already set for itself as a mission—a reason for being. The clearer this mission is to potential donors, the easier it will be to find them.

Let's take Habitat for Humanity, for example. Make a quick visit to its website and, in the course of thirty seconds or less, you will learn the essentials: "Habitat seeks to eliminate poverty housing and homelessness from the world and to make decent shelter a matter of conscience and action. [...] A Christian nonprofit, Habitat invites all people, everywhere, to build together in partnership."[5] Very quickly, you learn what Habitat does and the basis of its fundamental values. With a clear, compelling case and method, along with an unequalled track record, Habitat for Humanity International garners 70 percent of its support from individual donors, many of these being long-term, year-to-year investors, as well as volunteers.

## Practice Point

*Give your organization's mission statement a fresh read. As you read, do any natural donor constituencies emerge in your mind? Try to identify at least three.*

*Now, compare the three groupings you've identified to a list of your organization's current donors. How many fit into one of these natural categories? Is classification difficult? Use your answers and new understanding, to help you restructure your mission statement, donor acquisition programs or record keeping.*

### How do I find donors and identify what is important to them?

Remember the age-old aphorism, "birds of a feather flock together"? It certainly applies to fundraising. People give to what they want to support. Individuals invest in what they believe in. Appreciating this fact

**People give to what they want to support.**

will enable your organization to avoid two common fundraising fallacies, competing for donors and stealing donors, which are actually two sides of the same counterfeit coin. How often do you hear it said that

---

[5] Habitat for Humanity®. 15 June 2011. <http://www.habitat.org>.

competition for philanthropic revenue is increasing? Experience and research shows that philanthropy is not a fixed pie, but is elastic and dependent upon degrees of engagement by prospective donors within your organization.[6] Such a claim of "competition" only has validity to the extent that organizations approach their potential investors on a transactional basis—revenue-generating events that are based on buying and selling, for example. But the fact is that donors who willingly make investments in a particular charity because of deeply held values will not give equal attention to another organization with a dissimilar mission.

Some years ago, I worked with a large, multi-faceted charitable organization that had a well-developed major giving program, with a number of professional major gift officers. Several of these officers approached their work with this zero-sum perspective, with an attitude of, "I'll get mine before you make them yours." These officers, eager to get ahead of their peers and impress their superiors, would arbitrarily go into the prospective potential donor database and "assign" themselves to these prospects, thus "claiming" them for future gifts—all without any prior contact with the prospective donors It's ridiculous to think that the prospective donors, somehow, had no say in where they invested their philanthropic capital. These fundraisers were behaving as though donors were chess pieces to be moved around on the board.

This is not to say that individuals don't make casual gifts—even gifts that are made simply to get an over-zealous or tactless solicitor to "go away." Charitable gifts made from these perspectives are never capacity gifts—gifts that approach the donor's true giving ability—and are almost always "one-up gifts." Furthermore, arm-twisting potential

---

[6] Schervish, Paul G. "The Material Horizons of Philanthropy: New Directions for Money and Motives." *New Directions for Philanthropic Fundraising*. John Wiley & Sons, No. 29, November 2001.

donors into a gift carries serious risks that outweigh the benefits of any gift received. I once watched a very successful charitable organization conduct a large, comprehensive capital campaign using this "leave no prisoners" approach. The result? While money was raised and the chief development officer quickly landed a new, more prestigious position as a result of the organization's campaign "success," the organization was left with a landscape strewn with burned bridges that took a decade to rebuild.

So, how does your organization identify those who will invest in it? To identify potential donors, begin with the resources that are already at your organization's disposal. Board, staff and volunteers—especially volunteers—are all sources for potential donor referrals. Granted, some organizations have a simpler task than others in this regard. In fundraising parlance, churches have what is called a "closed constituency," whereas colleges and universities possess a "semi-open constituency." Simply stated, churches know who will support them—their members and regular attendees. Higher education looks principally to the alumni but also to parents and those who have a self-identified interested in education. Healthcare organizations garner support from the communities that they serve and from grateful patients. The vast array of social service and arts organizations have, more or less, what could be called an "open constituency."

Supporters of all organizations are driven by interest, affinity and mission—and, to a degree, proximity. The added difficulty in potential investor identification for open, or even semi-open, constituency organizations is that there is not a readily identifiable and defined group that can be considered potential donors. Still, this doesn't mean that identifying potential supporters is some sort of random search or a quest for the proverbial "needle in the haystack."

Here again, networks are king. Seth Godin uses the example that everyone is famous to 1,500 people.[7] Networks are so much more effective in identifying prospective donors than "broadcast" appeals. Both approaches, however, do have value and are typically used concurrently in an organization. Look to the places where potential donors identify *by their interests* and affinity for the mission of the organization. Certainly, professionally prepared mailing lists with appropriate filter criteria are good sources for the names of potential supporters. But, don't overlook other opportunities for "affinity groupings." Events and projects where like-minded people gather are also rich with prospect-mining potential.

### Practice Point

*Sophisticated direct mail marketing has made the process of identifying likely potential supporters to semi-open or open constituency organizations a great deal easier, less expensive and a lot more fruitful. The best results are achieved when direct mail is executed concurrently with an active "word-of-mouth" networking approach among known supporters.*

### What is the social profile of a donor? What key things should I look for in a donor profile?

In recent years, there has been a great deal of research conducted regarding consistent socio-economic, societal and behavioral variables that influence the propensity to give. The outcome of this research is readily available to even the smallest nonprofits and can be immensely useful in shaping a profile for their particular pool of potential donors.

---

[7] Godin, Seth. "Famous to the Family." Seth Godin's Blog. 9 March 2011.
< http://sethgodin.typepad.com/>.

There are a few constants, however, that are useful for any organization setting out to raise money. The single greatest factor which influences an individual's propensity to be philanthropic—to any organization— is whether he or she is a member or regular attendee of a church, synagogue or other community of faith.[8] The degree to which they are philanthropic is directly proportional to their commitment to their faith. This applies across the board and reflects the interest in giving to all charitable causes and organizations—not just to religion. This one fact can be extremely useful in helping you to quickly focus your attention upon prospective donors who have the best likelihood of being philanthropically inclined. When you combine this knowledge with the other primary points of your organizational "values" profile, much of the potential donor selection process is complete.

There are a number of other factors that influence philanthropic propensity, such as level of education, income, generational placement and whether the individual resides in an urban or rural community.[9] But while these factors have an impact, the overriding determinant as to whether an individual will be inclined to be philanthropic is his or her attitude toward, and participation in, religion. Factors other than religion tend to influence the *degree* of giving, rather than the *propensity* to give.

> **The single greatest factor which influences an individual's propensity to be philanthropic—to any organization—is whether he or she is a member or regular attendee of a church, synagogue or other community of faith.**

[8] "Social Capital Community Benchmark Survey (SCCBS)." Roper Center for Public Opinion Research. Saguaro Seminar at Harvard University.

[9] "Population Panel of Income Dynamics (PSID)." Detailed in the SCCBS. Center on Philanthropy at Indiana University; "General Social Survey (GSS)." National Opinion Research Center; "Generational Differences in Charitable Giving." Center on Philanthropy at Indiana University.

## *Practice Point*

*Being a member of a community of faith is the number one indicator of whether an individual will be philanthropic. Can you identify any others that are part of the "typical" donor profile for your organization? Is this profile merely assumed, or is it actually researched and born from experience? A quick check—although not a substitute for real donor research—is to take two or three of these social variables and then compare them to real donors. You may be surprised at what you discover.*

### What are the primary motivations and values people act upon to give money?

Let's look again at the word "philanthropy." If you recall, the English word comes from two Greek roots, "philio" and "anthropos," literally translated "brotherly affection" and "mankind." Philanthropy, then, is simply an active expression of "the brotherly love for humankind."

People make philanthropic gifts because they *want to*. They want to show their interest and affection for their fellow human beings. Whatever the method of soliciting a gift, the approach will, in some sense, build upon this common bond. Therefore, it makes common sense to adopt those approaches that develop the maximum connection between the gift, the giver and the common bond between people. This is why fundraising efforts that are built upon an organizational mission and appeal to fundamental human yearnings and need is far more effective—and lasting—than fundraising efforts that are merely commercial or social. Recall the outcome when the journalist polled those attending a charitable gala, described earlier. When there is little or no connection with the basic values of the donors, there is weak philanthropic intent and little or no loyalty.

## What are the top five motivations to give?

A number of studies have been conducted to identify and codify the primary motivations of donors—why individuals make gifts in the first place. Here in the United States, the five that occur most frequently among donors are individually, or in some combination:[10]

- To meet critical, basic needs
- To give back to society by making the community a better place
- A belief that those with more should help those with less
- To bring about a desired impact or result
- A request for money was made

Entire volumes could be (and, in some cases, have been) written, unpacking each of these reasons. Some commonly assumed motives—those with a primary self-interest, such as public recognition, business interests and charitable tax deduction—are actually not very common at all. These "self-interest" motives are important to only 5 percent or less of donors.[11]

Look at the last item on the list—simply being asked. The part of fundraising that most people shy away from is the *asking*. And yet, without it, most gifts would never be made. You must ask.

Although asking is essential, it is actually a relatively small part of the fundraising process, as we shall see. The irony here is that so much of fundraising is seen as "sell, close, get," that there is the common

---

[10] "Understanding Donors' Motivations." Center on Philanthropy at Indiana University, 2009; "Study of High Net-Worth Philanthropy." Center on Philanthropy at Indiana University, 2009; "Generational Differences in Charitable Giving." Center on Philanthropy at Indiana University.

[11] "Study of High Net-Worth Philanthropy." Center on Philanthropy at Indiana University, 2009.

misunderstanding that asking is the sum total of the process. Asking isn't demanding, however. It isn't even cajoling. It certainly isn't legitimized begging. Asking gives potential donors an opportunity to invest in a worthy organization or undertaking that is in concert with their most fundamental values. It's nothing less than an opportunity for self-realization. Wow.

So, there are two precursors to creating a workable fundraising plan for your organization:

1. Determine who your potential supporters are by evaluating both the financial ability and personal affinity of your "suspects"—those individuals whom you *suspect* may be prospective donors but who have not yet had both affinity and ability confirmed.

2. Understand the particular motivations; this will allow you to identify what drives them to give freely to your organization.

Principle 5: Work From the Inside Out, and Principle 6: Divide & Grow, are the natural next steps in the process and together form the core of the active fundraising process.

### *Practice Point*

*Identify the top five reasons repeat donors give to your organization. How did you determine these reasons? Are they validated or assumed? If they can be validated, are these reasons encouraged and supported through your organization's outreach to these donors? For instance, if your donors give to you because your organization is effective in its mission, do all of your communications emphasize this mission, either directly or indirectly?*

*If you have never conducted independent and/or primary
research on your donor base, it would be of immeasurable value and
would return much more in increased—and sustained—
giving than it costs. Such research would help you look at the
organization from the donors' perspectives and shape content and
communication that appeals to the reasons donors support you in
the first place. Of course, this assumes that the results
of the research are put into action.*

## What causes people to make gifts?

There seems to be so much focus on *how* one makes a gift that the *why* is often overlooked. Give by check, give by credit card, give by automatic debit and even give by text message. Give cash, give stocks, make a will, organize a trust and take an annuity. The list goes on. All of these things are well and good—useful in their places. But they do not get to the root of why a gift is made in the first place. No one invests in a charitable organization because they were impressed with a clever financial mechanism or payment scheme or charmed by a "slick" appeal. Such things may, and sometimes do, influence the amount and/or timing of a gift. They are not primary motivators.

Giving is fundamentally both a *rational* and an *irrational* act. Head and heart. Dispassion and passion. Left and right brain. In this equation, the irrational almost always leads, with the rational giving support and guidance to the decision. An effective, successful gift solicitation is crafted to be meaningful to the donor by appealing to his or her particular set of emotions and rational calculations.

## Currently at the Coeur d'Alene Center for the Arts

As the September board meeting approaches, Jane has asked Lauren to draft a revised fundraising operating plan for the next fiscal year. This plan will begin to address the long-term need of building a strong program of individual giving, as well as moving away from the current heavy dependence on event revenue, while minimizing the potential impact of lost event revenue in the transition. As Lauren stares at a blank piece of paper, she is wondering just where to begin...and where the "limits" really are.

The annual fundraising plan for the center really hasn't changed much in almost ten years. Rather than a cohesive plan of interdependent efforts, which work together to provide a core base of philanthropic income and revenue growth, the current plan is really a "to-do list." It's a line-item list of the various independent efforts that have been a part of the fundraising landscape at the center for quite some time. And why change it? It's worked well enough in the past. Isn't fundraising all about cash-in, anyway?

In their first meeting, Jane and Lauren struggled to establish an overall direction that could be sold to the board. "Can we really ask the board to step up and be a meaningful part of this effort, and will they?" openly wondered Jane. Jane has been the executive director for six years and has developed some credibility with the board—especially the newer members. How much political capital can she expend on this effort? Where does Jack, the board chair, fit in all of this?

During their first meeting, Lauren suggested that the two *really* didn't know much about their donors, why they support the center or even their financial abilities to give.

"What do you mean?" quipped Jane. "We know that our donors continue to support us each year because they're pleased with our programs."

"Are they?" responded Lauren.

Continuing to relate current assumptions about the CACA's donors, Jane pointed out that the "old-timers" on the board—those who were a part of its founding—have been tied to the community for years and, through their efforts, have developed a set of activities and efforts that the community has responded well to for over 30 years. Lauren didn't dispute this fact, but she returned to her questions once again, "What do our donors *really* want, and what makes them continue to support us from year to year? What *could* our donors give?"

Jane continued to look at Lauren blankly, until Lauren made reference to the elephant in the room: the rate of minting new donors has been slowly decreasing for the last three to four years. Let's explore how Principle 4: Learn & Plan might help Jane and Lauren address this issue.

## Questions to Consider

1. How is Principle 4: Learn & Plan shaping what is happening to the center's fundraising?

2. What's the best approach for a course correction— aggressive or gentle?  How?

3. What are the missing components to this puzzle? What should the CACA's leadership add to their tool kit?

4. How quickly should Jane and Lauren bring the board into the planning process, and what should the board's role be?

# Principle 5

# Work from the Inside Out

"Proxumus sum egomet mihi."
(Charity begins at home.)
— Terence

Whether seeking another's help or to share good news, we naturally go to those we are closest to. Why? Because they *know* us, and we know them. Trust, at some level, exists between us. It is the same with fundraising that looks to build long-term investor relationships, and Principle 5: Work from the Inside Out demonstrates this aspect of human behavior. By starting from the inside, we are more likely to build relationships with new supporters as the "network of influence" grows.

### What is working from the inside out?

Working from the "inside out" is, quite simply, building financial support first among those who have the closest relationship with your organization. Think of it as building concentric circles of support for your organization, beginning with those who, by their current relationship to the organization, formally or informally, are the best informed and most committed.

### Why should I work from the inside out?

Working from the inside out accomplishes two aims. First and foremost, you are asking those with the best reasons to give. When you're looking to build new relationships, nothing speaks higher of your organization than the solid support of those who are already engaged. This is precisely why board members should be the "lead" donors in any organization. They do not necessarily have to be the *largest* donors, but they must always be the *first*.

**Board members should be the "lead" donors in any organization.**

The paid staff members of your organization are the other "most inside" group. These individuals draw their livelihood from the organization and have, perhaps, the most vested interest. A high level of donor participation among the staff of your organization builds commitment and *esprit de corps* like nothing else. As with other donors, it's all about commensurate giving—what is possible and appropriate for each person.

Employee solicitation, although straightforward, is operationally specific and distinct, requiring appropriate training. If your organization has never approached staff members for gifts in a systematic and comprehensive way, bringing in an outside consultant or experienced development officer might serve you well. You want your first effort of staff solicitation to be a positive experience for all involved.

### Practice Point

*Consider what board and staff giving looks like at your organization. What percentage of board and staff members give? Is the solicitation of these individuals organized and done on a regular basis, with a timeline and goal? Or, is it just an "understood" commitment, with board and staff members giving passively as the mood strikes, without being directly or purposefully asked to give? Do the giving amounts reflect the true financial ability of those giving? The answers to these questions should be your focus as you assess the level of financial commitment of your board and staff.*

### Why are the "usual suspects" not always the best donors?

Ever since Claude Rains uttered the immortal line, "Round up the usual suspects," in the film *Casablanca*, this statement has encapsulated how conventional fundraising wisdom often misguides our efforts and obscures the facts. In fundraising, the "usual suspects" are typically visible people in the community who have apparent wealth or position and may or may not be philanthropic. Their relationship with your organization might be nothing more than living in the same community or being the friend of a friend.

**There are lots of wealthy, even generous, people who will never give your organization a dime— and for valid reasons.**

Remember that an individual that has the potential to be a donor to your organization must possess two qualities: an ability to give and an affinity to your organization. Ability to give is, hopefully, obvious. Affinity is a bit subtler and often overlooked. Identification with your organization's general goals and values constitutes a base level of affinity. There are lots of wealthy, even generous, people who will never give your organization a dime—and for valid reasons. They don't have the same interests, they don't have a relationship with your organization and/or they are simply not philanthropic in their outlook. Even the most visible philanthropists in a community aren't necessarily potential donors to *your* organization. They simply may not have interests that coincide with the goals of your organization. Moreover, by being visible, they are on everyone's list. As a result, they often have to be *even more* selective in the charities they support.

### Practice Point

*Does your organization distinguish between "ability" and "affinity" in its donors? If so, does it track these attributes and use them to develop successful solicitation approaches?*

*In tracking these attributes, the levels of ability and affinity are most effectively identified and recorded using some sort of donor software. The program will assign "scores," which should then be used to determine the manner, timing and solicitation amounts. If your organization is not using this method of tracking, what does your organization use to identify whom to solicit first, and for how much? Is it working?*

## Where do I start?

Think of a set of concentric circles, the "rock in the pond." What set of individuals form the tightest, most intimate circle of relationship with your organization? Volunteer leaders, beginning with board members and staff form the tightest inner circle.

> **Pure altruism will never compensate for a real or perceived lack of commitment by the organization's leadership and staff.**

Board members set the direction of the organization, approve budgets and determine programs. Staff members provide the creative direction and idea implementation. They also derive their livelihood from the organization. Who better to be donors and ensure the organization's future than these individuals?

It's simply axiomatic to human behavior. Why would potential donors give to an organization that does not have the firm financial support of those charged with the well-being of the organization and, moreover, those who draw their incomes from the organization? Pure altruism will never compensate for a real or perceived lack of commitment by the organization's leadership and staff.

I worked with the executive director of a small organization that was seeking to place itself on firm financial footing. Trying to get the board's attention at a board meeting, the executive director commented that organizational finances were so tenuous that the "curtains [were] on fire." At that meeting, I pointed to the board as the place to begin.

That's when enthusiasm for a serious fundraising program began to wane. "Maybe we don't need a fundraising plan but a marketing plan," was one board member's response. The fundraising plan was shelved and significant funds—especially sizable given the organization's budget—were spent on a marketing and "image" study, where only business representatives were interviewed. "Change the name," was the recommendation. The name change was dutifully made. The executive director was instructed to "go out and find it." The board bemoaned a lackluster economy. Finally, there came the endless rounds of galas and auctions. The organization struggled then…and continues to do so today. The board members, unfortunately, continue to look everywhere, anywhere, for funding—to anything or anyone other than themselves. The truly disappointing fact about this tale of woe is that there are entirely too many other nonprofits who continue to struggle with leadership; sadly, they prefer to begin their fundraising efforts with those in the outer circles, rather than with those on the inside.

### *Practice Point*

*Have you ever found yourself in a situation where you were committed to giving that was commensurate to your ability, but your peers in leadership were not? If so, how did you feel? What was your reaction—anger, passive resignation, indifference? If you are still a member of that organization's board, has your giving commitment moved to match that of your peers, or has their commitment moved closer to yours? In answering these questions, consider how you can set an example to others in your organization, including the staff.*

## What is the paradigm of "equal sacrifice vs. equal dollars"?

I am often asked the question as to what board members and staff should give. Many organizations attempt to settle this question by establishing some sort of uniform minimum, either as a percentage of members who give gifts or a uniform giving amount. So, for example, 75 percent of all board members should make a gift or all board members are asked to each give $1,000. As to the percentage of board and staff who give, it should be 100 percent. Period. As to the level of financial commitment, we need to recognize that giving ability among board and staff members will not be uniform. An established, uniform giving expectation will always be a challenge for some and an after-thought for others.

Much more meaningful to everyone involved is applying the principle of equal sacrifice rather than equal dollars. In this manner, a strong commitment is developed among all board members, both to the organization and each other. Such an approach also allows for boards to be peopled with individuals other than simply those with deep pockets. Your governing board needs to be representative of the principal giving constituencies that support your organization. Such representation makes possible the most effective fundraising program, while also providing critical legitimacy and acceptance within the community your organization serves. Certainly, boards will differ as to the giving ability among their members; nevertheless, there is often significant differential in giving ability among even the wealthiest of boards. Moreover, by requiring equal sacrifice, more money will be raised and will set the strongest possible example for existing and potential donors.

## Practice Point

*What is the true aggregate financial giving ability of your governing board? Use your organization's annual fund, the yearly cash giving program that seeks general operating gifts, as an example. Take a piece of paper and create a list of all of the members of your organization's board.*

*Starting at the top of the list, consider each name and answer the question, "What could (insert name) contribute this year in a cash gift if (he/she) was properly motivated to do so?" Notice that the question is not what you think the particular board member will do; instead, it is what he or she is capable of doing, if properly motivated.*

*If estimating such a number seems daunting, or even a bit like witchcraft, don't worry. Assigning asking amounts for individual donors for the first time can seem impossible, and your organization may even be new to the concept of the "specific ask." Over time, though, you will learn this skill. Using a consultant to guide you through this process the first few times can help speed up the learning process.*

*Once you've done this for every name on your list, add up the amounts and compare the sum with the known aggregate giving by your board in the most recent year. If the total of actual giving doesn't reach at least 60–70 percent of the potential ability (the sum on your chart), your organization has some serious work to do with regard to building board commitment and strength.*

**What does this mean for staff members? Why do staff members need to be donors?**

All of this means that staff members are not exempt from the need to give and that they, too, should be evaluated on their ability to give when asked. The amount of money raised here is almost always significantly less than that raised

> **When staff members become donors, they become true stockholders.**

from board members, but the principle is the same. Strengthening your organization's commitment to fundraising and maximizing sustainable outcomes comes from engaging existing and potential donors at the highest possible levels, beginning with those who have the most to gain. It's inside out.

When staff members become donors, they become true stockholders. They understand and appreciate the need for financial support in a personal way, and they are far more likely to be fully engaged in, and subsequently endorse, the strategic direction of the organization. They may even become involved in the fundraising process at some level.

### *Practice Point*

*Examine the state of staff giving in your organization. Is there an organized program and an option for payroll deduction? Do staff members feel like they are a part of the fundraising process? Likewise, are they seen as partners and a critical part of fundraising success? Is fundraising a part of your organization's culture—something equally important as its primary mission? If not, is fundraising seen as somehow independent of everything else—or worse—as a necessary evil?*

There is a direct and proportional correlation between the level of acceptance of fundraising as a part of an organization's culture and the level of staff giving. I like to say that fundraising is not a spectator sport. Everyone is on the playing field and not on the benches. To be effective and sustained, fundraising initiatives must be seen as what your organization "does" as much as the actual services and/or programs it provides.

How does one solicit an organization's board? The most effective and transformative way to solicit board members is what is called "peer solicitation." Stated simply, board members solicit each other, face-to-face, using an "asking" amount that is appropriate for each member. Giving level "peers" ask each other after the solicitor has made his or her own gift, of course. If your organization doesn't have experience with this approach, the assistance of a qualified consultant can be of immeasurable value.

---

### Why are *all* gifts important?

All gifts, from the smallest and most modest to the largest and most spectacular, are important and essential. Veteran fundraisers will tell you that the distribution of gifts in any fundraising program follows a predictable pattern. The Pareto Principle, if you recall, says that approximately 80 percent of the funds raised will come from about 20 percent of those giving. Depending upon the situation and organization, that ratio can be more like 90/10 or higher. This is donor behavior that is shown to be consistent over time, place and organization.

So, why not go after the "fat cats" and dispense with the "small guys"? After all, fundraising costs money and resources are scarce. It sounds like a plan. That is, until you realize that all gifts form a cohesive whole for the support of an organization; they're all interdependent. Board and staff giving provide needed organizational endorsement, especially for the potential donors of significant ability. The large gifts drive that endorsement home to the community. It is the more modest— even very modest—gifts, however, that provide the *legitimacy* that an organization must possess, both among those it garners support from and those it serves. An organization that does not have sufficiently broad community support and recognition will not last for long. Beyond this, even modest gifts amount to real money.

On a knoll in central Kentucky, within a portion of the farm purchased in 1808 by Abraham Lincoln's father, Thomas Lincoln, stands a Beaux Arts classical granite and marble building. Inside this building is a log cabin similar to the cabin in which the 16th President of the United States was born. Leading up to that structure are fifty-six steps, one for each year in Lincoln's life. The cornerstone of that building was laid by President Theodore Roosevelt in 1909 and, subsequently, dedicated by President Taft in 1911. It was the "penny" donations of thousands upon thousands of American school children, however, that financed the memorial's construction. Small gifts do matter. All gifts matter.

### *Practice Point*

*Every charitable organization has its own giving distribution profile—it's interpretation of the Pareto Principle (80/20). The giving "pyramid" tends to be steeper, with fewer donors and larger gifts for arts organizations and flatter, with more donors making smaller gifts for youth and social service organizations, for example. Develop your organization's pyramid by taking it's gifting data for a year and organizing it by number of gifts for each gift size (10 gifts of $1, 5 gifts of $5, etc.)*

*Next, create a similar pyramid for each of the last five years.*
*Is the gift distribution remaing relatively stable over the time*
*period? Is it getting steeper with few donors giving more?*
*Is it getting flatter with more donors each giving less?*
*All gifts are important and you want to make sure that your*
*organization is garnering support from its entire potential*
*constituency. This is the way to ensure that you are approaching*
*your organization's natural and true fundraising potential.*

## Currently at the Coeur d'Alene Center for the Arts

Although the board and staff members of the CACA aren't really "asked" to give, they do. Roughly 70 percent of the board members make a gift annually out of personal funds. "How many give something that actually reflects their respective *abilities* to give?" thought Lauren. In preparation for her initial planning meeting with Jane, Lauren took a list of the current board members and, one by one, asked herself the question, "What could this person give if they were properly motivated to do so?" She was not really surprised, by the result. According to her evaluation, only one board member was making an unsolicited gift that roughly reflected his giving capacity as Lauren had estimated it. "It could be worse," she thought. Not by much. Such an outcome isn't unusual, given the manner in which the board members make their gifts.

As she developed her new and revised plan to present to Jane, Lauren knew instinctively that the greatest potential for impact on the fundraising bottom line lay within the board. She knew that, at a minimum, she needed 100 percent participation in giving among board members; she also recognized that to go to the "next level," she needed gift sizes that made sense for each person. The question was how to go about it.

Like their board member counterparts, staff members have always been given the *opportunity* to give through the availability of payroll deduction, but they have never been *asked* to give. While Jane and Lauren make small monthly gifts through their paychecks, other staff members don't participate; they will gladly participate in the fundraising events, sometimes making modest purchases.

The CACA has relied heavily on volunteers during its entire existence—literally hundreds of them over the center's thirty-year plus history. From classroom helpers and adjunct faculty for the plethora of educational opportunities to the many assistants that are needed to help with exhibitions and performances, a considerable number of people in Coeur d'Alene and the surrounding community have participated in some way. Until now, there has never been a connection between volunteering to help in the CACA's work and whether an individual is asked for a gift. If there are intersections between those in the annually purchased mass market mailing list and the group of volunteers, that's fine, but it certainly isn't purposeful. Frankly, no one has ever thought about asking volunteers for a donation.

The CACA board members are well-connected in the Coeur d'Alene community, and although there is considerable overlap in their circles of influence, they know a *lot* of people. In the past, Jane has suggested that one of the ways the CACA could enlarge its base of support would be for board members to tap their professional and personal networks. The response has been predictable: most board members suggested Jacob Arnot and Harriet Simmons—the "usual suspects." Harriet and Jacob are the chieftains of Coeur d'Alene's "old guard" and have consistently underwritten much of the serious philanthropy in the community for half a century. Both Jacob and Harriet have been approached by those representing the center and can be counted on to support it—to a point.

During Jane and Lauren's most recent visit with Jacob this past spring, he was asked to move up from his long-time position as a mid-level sponsor of the summer art auction—the Art Extravaganza—to the top spot, filling the newly formed gap left by the withdrawal of the leading community bank. He respectfully declined, pointing out that he is being approached by more charities for more money each and every year. He even confided that he's beginning to feel a bit overwhelmed, saying that he's frustrated that most of those seeking his support continually try to sell him something, rather than outright asking for a gift—and building a case for that. Jacob added that, although he supports the center because he believes in enhancing the cultural wellbeing of the community, his first love, after the synagogue, is a local hospital that once saved the life of his late wife, Rachel, over thirty years ago. This was all new information for both Jane and Lauren. Neither of them knew of his past relationship with the hospital or that he was Jewish and active in his synagogue.

Jacob concluded his meeting with Lauren and Jane by suggesting that they be a bit more deliberate in identifying and cultivating the "new money" in the community, as there had been a period of moneyed growth in the area during the past decade, prior to the most recent economic downturn. Pondering how to proceed, both Jane and Lauren left Jacob's office that day separately convinced that the members of the board are their current best hope to enlarge the effective giving networks of the center. But how to do it? Let's look at how Principle 5: Work from the Inside Out might help answer this question.

## Questions to Consider

1. How is Principle 5: Work from the Inside Out influencing the future of the CACA?  What are its current points of impact?

2. How might board members be encouraged to make yearly gifts that reflect their true giving abilities?

3. Should Jacob Arnot be asked to help with his suggestion of seeking "new money"?

4. What are the downsides to simply maintaining the status quo?

# Principle 6

# Divide & Grow

"When you come to a fork in the road, take it."
— Yogi Berra

I am blessed with a number of friends and colleagues from many walks of life and places across the country. I value all of these individuals and the relationships we share, but I recognize that they are all different. Their personal interests vary. Their skills and talents vary. Their needs vary. Even my relationship with each individual varies. When I look to build a base of support for a project on which I am working I, quite naturally, assemble that group of colleagues that are in the best position to help that particular project succeed.

It's the same with fundraising relationships. Principle 6: Divide & Grow describes how donors come in all shapes and sizes, as well as explains how to build lasting relationships with investors. While all donors are important and necessary to the success of an organization, each has a role to play in the fundraising drama.

**What are the four building blocks, or tasks, necessary to engage donors? How do I move donors from initial gifts to major gifts?**

Building lasting relationships that are productive for both donors and your organization is essential for a fundraising program that is sustainable over time. The intricacies and nuances of donor relationships are often made complex; however, the essence of relationship building is captured in four essential tasks. Your organization must acquire new donors, it must retain those donors at the highest possible rate. It must move them, over time, to their highest possible levels of giving and finally, it must coordinate all these efforts as it reaches out to investors and potential donors.

> Your organization must acquire new donors, it must retain those donors at the highest possible rate, it must move them, over time, to their highest possible levels of giving and finally, it must coordinate all these efforts as it reaches out to investors and potential donors.

To visualize this process, think of it as a pipeline. Donors are moved along the relational path with your organization, purposefully and consistently but at their own pace. A simple chart on the following page, the Donor Progression Pipeline, illustrates the "pipeline." Beginning at the left, your organization must have a vehicle or program to acquire new donors, an ability to get someone to give to you for the first time (see chart, "Donor Acquisition"). Next, and most importantly, you must retain as many of those first-time donors as possible. Although retaining *all* of your first-time donors just isn't possible, for a variety of reasons, without high donor retention, your organization's fundraising totals will be comprised of only entry-level gifts (see Donor Progression Pipeline, "Donor Retention & Progression"). First-time gifts are almost always a fraction of a particular donor's giving ability. It's the rare investor that places his or her entire portfolio into an organization that is unknown or untested to them. From an established pool of ongoing investors who give each year, your organization needs to identify donors who have the ability and propensity to make more significant cash gifts. These larger cash gifts, usually four and five figures, will supply your organization with a significant, if not the majority, portion of the ongoing, current operating cash it receives. Gifts in this range typically commence between the third and fifth gift a donor makes to your organization. This assumes that the donor is financially capable, the donor's giving is renewed annually and the donor is brought closer to the organization through appropriate acknowledgment and appreciation efforts.

From your organization's group of "high cash" donors, a pool of prospective investors for "major gifts" can be developed (see Donor Progression Pipline). A major gifts program is a fundraising initiative to identify, cultivate, grow and subsequently solicit a pool of investors with the potential to make a gift from their assets rather than income.

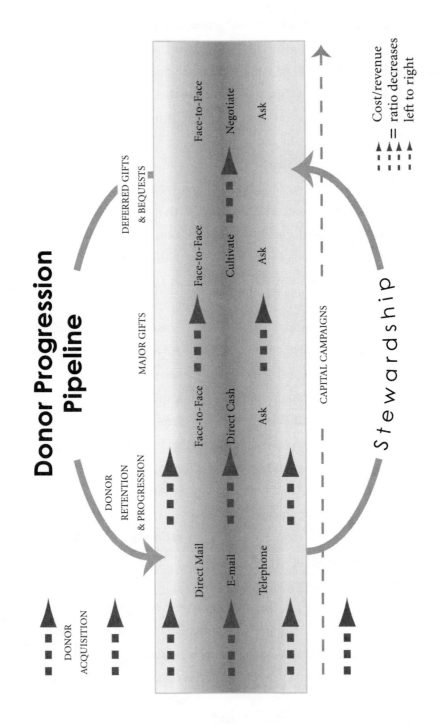

# Donor Progression Pipeline

I often work with clients who express a desire to get into soliciting "major gifts." Their use of the term sometimes means simply "bigger" gifts—gifts that are significant simply due to their size. The monetary level that defines whether a gift is major will vary depending upon your organization. For the donor and your specific fundraising program, the distinction here is not the absolute size of the gift but that the donor makes such a gift out of his or her assets rather than income. A gift such as this signals, yet again, a higher level of commitment to the organization than regular, even high-level, cash gifts made from income. Major gifts are usually given for specific purposes. The purpose of a major gift is mutually negotiated between the donor and your organization and is usually formalized through some sort of pledge agreement, which is typically satisfied over a period of three to five years.

The final section of the development or fundraising pipeline is a program or vehicle devoted to obtaining "planned" or "deferred" gifts (see Donor Progression Pipeline, "Deferred Gifts & Bequests"). Although they can be operationally and legally complex, these gifts are—from a donor's point of view—major gifts for which fulfillment is deferred in some manner to achieve a secondary objective of the donor, often unrelated to the charitable organization itself. Take, for example, a couple who owned a 6,000-acre ranch in the Rockies. Hardworking and unassuming, as are many ranchers, this couple was very devoted to a particular charitable organization that they have supported for decades. Wanting to make a substantial gift and lacking great liquidity, they were encouraged to consider a charitable remainder unitrust (CRUT). The couple was pleased to learn that with a CRUT, they could gift the ranch to the organization (in which the heirs had no interest), avoid a significant capital gains tax (which they would have incurred if the ranch had been merely sold), receive a lifetime income and be able to take a charitable deduction for the ranch, as well as a deduction for a portion of the subsequent income. The charitable organization retains the asset, the ranch. This opportunity came as a revelation to this couple; they were able to make a transformative gift and, at the same time, provide for themselves later in life.

Major donors—donors who give out of assets—can, and often do, continue to be high-end cash donors. Major donors will often make planned gifts, as well. Planned gifts, because of their deferred nature and secondary benefits, are made by donors who have insufficient cash flow or asset liquidity to be high-end cash givers or make major gifts. Such donors often have long-term loyalty to your organization making modest gifts, sometimes for decades.

The pipeline is cemented together and reinforced by an ongoing program of donor stewardship. "Stewardship" is fundraising-speak for those activities that are related to meaningful communication, appreciation and recognition of your organization's donors. Capital or endowment campaigns, while being quite successful at providing significant funds over a relatively short period of time for a specific project or projects, also serve to expand the base-level of giving and broaden the donor pool of your organization (represented by the "Capital Campaigns" arrow on the pipeline).

Donor progression, or movement, within the pipeline is left to right—from initially modest gifts, to larger cash gifts, to a relationship characterized by gifts of assets and finally, the planned distribution of those assets to your organization. A pipeline that is virtually seamless from the donor's perspective, ensuring a high level of coordination between the various fundraising programs, is essential to sustainable fundraising. Such a pipeline enables the organization to build a meaningful relationship with a donor that achieves maximum longevity and fundraising productivity.

At this point, you're probably thinking, "But what about donors whose first gift is a major or planned gift?" Occasionally, a donor will appear and make a significant gift without any apparent prior involvement with

**Generous people make bequests all the time.**

your organization. It does happen, but it is a rare occurence. Gifts of significant size, which arrive without any prior effort on your organization's part, can also carry with them conditions or restrictions that make the gift a lot less appealing. Finally, despite their immediate value to the organization, these gifts are almost always not repeatable.

Take, for example, the unexpected bequest. A couple of years ago, an article appeared in a city daily, which related the events surrounding the unexpected bequest to three local charities from a recently deceased couple. The thrust of the article was how unusual and unexpected the bequest was. That isn't what struck my eye, however. Generous people make bequests all the time. Remember, bequests account for about 8 percent of all philanthropy in America each year.

What caught my attention was the reported response of the three charities that were the beneficiaries of the largess. One executive director commented that the bequest would enable his organization to "keep the lights on." Another said that the organization could continue to "run for a year longer." Two of the three recipients didn't even know the donor couple when they were alive. As these nonprofits illustrate, a strong fundraising platform is not in place when organizations are dependent upon unexpected deaths to continue to operate. Those types of gifts have the odds of the lottery.

The couple in question, obviously motivated to give back, potentially could have been long-term partners of the organizations that shared their values—if only those organizations had reached out to them in their lifetime. An unexpected bequest is more than a windfall; it is also a missed opportunity.

## *Practice Point*

*Using the Donor Progression Pipeline as a guide, examine how your organization uses the four building blocks to engaging donors (acquisition, retention, progression and coordination). Can you identify at least one program that addresses, in some way, each of the four building blocks? Do the fundraising programs in your organization each have a clear purpose that supports an overarching strategy, or are they simply independent, disconnected vehicles to "raise money"?*

*Consider if any of the four building blocks are not being adequately addressed in your organization's current fundraising program. Can the existing fundraising vehicles be adapted so that they support a long-term strategy? If not, is it time to revamp your programs and strategies?*

## What is the myth of "competition"?

We often hear how the proliferation of charitable organizations is increasing the competition for philanthropic funds, thus making fundraising increasingly difficult with diminishing returns on fundraising programs. Such an assertion is a myth and a variation on the old theme, "If you get yours, I won't get mine."

This myth is supported by two principal assertions that (1) charitable gifts comprise a fixed, static pool of available funds and (2) organizations "convince" or "persuade" the donor through push marketing techniques, rather than the donor making a value-based decision. Both of these assertions are false.

Research has shown that, far from being a fixed pool of available funds, philanthropy is extremely elastic.[12] In practical terms, any theoretical limit isn't even close to being approached. Furthermore, it is the individual donor, rather than the organization, that decides where to invest—Principle 1: Donors are the Drivers in action. Donors make these decisions on the basis of their values and

> **Your organization will only be in competition for philanthropic funding if it fails to distinguish itself from other nonprofits.**

select organizations that have values and goals similar to their own. The degree to which an organization is in competition with another is only with regard to organizations with a similar mission. Then, the competition is not for an artificially fixed donor pool but rather on the basis of which organization is more effective in fulfilling its mission. Your organization will only be in competition for philanthropic funding if it fails to distinguish itself from other nonprofits. This is yet another reason why transactional fundraising, fundraising built around a material exchange, is such a killer—not only does it lower the financial sights of donors, but it does so without leading with a mission. Thus, fundraising becomes simply a "buying and selling" exercise for all nonprofits.

## Practice Point

*Think about whether your organization has ever been in "competition" with another nonprofit. If so, how could your organization's mission statement be fine-tuned or your outcomes more clearly distinguished to address the "competition"? Consider whether there are any nonprofits you might join forces with in some way, either through an outright merger, coordination or division of efforts.*

---

[12] Schervish, Paul G. *The Material Horizons of Philanthropy: New Directions for Money and Motives.* New Directions for Philanthropic Fundraising. John Wiley & Sons, No. 29, November 2001.

*Within your own organization, do you see a zero-sum attitude in staff representing the various programs? If so, how can you effectively deal with this?*

## How does the constituency divide itself?

Although development professionals talk a great deal about, and spend a considerable amount of effort on, dividing or "segmenting" the donor base into various groupings, it's the donors who do the "dividing"—all on their own. Your organization's task is simply to identify those groups. Remember Principle 1: Donors are the Drivers. Good fundraising practice simply recognizes the distinctions and variations that already exist among donors and builds a program to accommodate and develop donors based upon those distinctions. These divisions are built upon criteria related to "affinity" and "ability." Affinity is the character and depth of the relationship that the donor has with your organization. Ability is the donor's financial ability to give. Remember, for an individual to be considered a prospective investor, they must possess both. By understanding the nature of the relationship a particular donor has with your organization, as well as his or her financial profile, you can construct a fundraising program that will be both meaningful to the donor and productive for your organization.

> **Affinity is the character and depth of the relationship that the donor has with your organization. Ability is the donor's financial ability to give.**

## Why doesn't a uniform giving approach work?

How often have you heard someone offer a solution to a fundraising project that goes something like this: "All we need to do is ask 100 people for $100 each, and will raise the $10,000 we need." This would sound like wisdom was it not for something called the Pareto Principle. Some people will, indeed, give the $100 asked of them. Some will give $50. Others will give $5. And then there are those who will give nothing at all—so much for getting $100 across the board. Attempting to meet a fundraising goal through uniform, equal giving amounts is doomed to failure. It simply doesn't work. Remember: regardless of how you solicit funds for a project, about 80 percent of the amount given will come from around 20 percent of those giving. By asking someone who could give $1,000 toward a $10,000 project for a gift of $100, you have immediately dismissed 90 percent of that donor's potential; furthermore, nine other individuals who have the ability to make a $100 gift now have to make up the difference. As you can see, using such an approach causes you to quickly run out of possible donors. Hopefully, this is sufficient for you to be dissuaded from attempting to raise funds using a uniform giving approach.

### *Practice Point*

*How can your organization shift from the "average giving" model? Consider how you might counter a push to use a "one-size-fits-all" giving approach the next time it surfaces. What alternative will you propose in its place?*

*How will you utilize the natural donor constituencies to suggest a more realistic giving approach?*

**How can I design individualized programs for each constituency?**

At this point, you may be wondering how your organization can design and implement a fundraising program that will appeal to and engage donors who vary greatly by giving inclination, financial ability and age. Designing such a program is straightforward. Implementing it has traditionally been the challenge, especially for smaller nonprofits. The advent of the PC and powerful pre-packaged software products and services has leveled the playing field, bringing sophisticated, comprehensive fundraising tools within the reach of just about every nonprofit organization. By acquiring a comprehensive donor management software suite, for example, your nonprofit can divide and grow the donor constituency in as finely delineated segments as it would like.

Any fundraising program is only as good as the data that drives it. I continue to marvel at the number of nonprofits, of all sizes, who do not make maintaining accurate (and I do mean accurate) addresses of their donors and potential donors a priority. The address maintenance function used by many organizations is simply return mail through the postal service. Such an approach for updating your organization's database is extremely costly, slow and not even all that accurate or complete. As a result, many nonprofits are routinely communicating with only a fraction of those *of whom they know* have a relationship or interests similar to theirs.

Conducting a regular address screen is one of the simplest things your nonprofit can do to maintain contact with those donors and potential donors it already knows. What good are sophisticated, direct marketing programs (which can be very effective) if the names identified as a result of those efforts are not maintained as "active"? There are a number of commercial firms that provide these services at a reasonable cost.

Determining the giving capacity and level of affinity of a donor base has long been the responsibility of the tried-and-true prospect review committee. A group of volunteers convene to confidentially review names and attempt to assign giving capacities and interest levels for an annual or capital campaign—even for a lifetime of giving. This approach to donor research is very effective in situations where people know one another reasonably well and the donors are relatively well-connected to your organization. Electronic donor pool wealth and income screens, performed by a donor research agency, have come a long way since their inception in the early 1990s, and many of these products are now quite sophisticated. What's more, as the quality and functionality of these tools have increased, the cost has declined rather substantially, making them available to nonprofits of virtually any size. While certainly not always accurate, nor a complete answer to your organization's donor research needs, such an instrument—chosen wisely—can go a long way in getting a sense of the size, breadth and potential of your donor and/or potential donor pool.

As you begin to identify the natural groupings of your donor constituency, always ask yourself, "Why is this donor or potential donor on the list?" Take nothing for granted. Always question a conventional assumption. Untested or inherited assumptions are some of the most lethal assassins of effective fundraising.

Last, but certainly not least, on the "infrastructure" list, is the presence of a staff member who is assigned the task of managing the fundraising process or program at your nonprofit. A qualified development professional certainly fits the bill, but depending on the size of your organization, such a person may not yet be affordable. Whether the incumbent is someone with basic skills and aptitude or a seasoned professional, the job description that this individual will fulfill in your organization is even more important than the person who fills it.

113

When I am working with a client organization and ask what the person assigned to "fundraising" does, I get very different answers: "He writes grants." "She organizes events." "He accepts gifts and mails acknowledgments." "She does marketing." All of these responses belie a basic misunderstanding of the fundraising process as I have been describing it. True, writing grants is part of fundraising. Certainly, events—properly designed and delivered—are important and can be effective. The word "marketing" is so general that it can mean anything from a corporate sponsorship program to promoting the actual services of the charitable organization to obtaining general media attention—hardly fundraising.

When I use the term "fundraiser" or "development officer," I am referring to the individual who is charged with managing the fundraising process in its entirety, using Principle 1: Donors are the Drivers, while ensuring the integrity of the donor pipeline. The effective fundraiser has his or her eye on the entire process as they engage and motivate volunteers and donors—from the board members outward to the most modest, first-time donor.

A healthy investment in infrastructure always returns far more than it costs. A common mistake that nonprofits make, however, is pursuing a false economy by focusing on initial cost alone without proper consideration for long-term benefits or usability. In addition to hampering an organization's fundraising efforts, an over focus on economy can have other unintended results. I was serving as counsel to a small, but respected nonprofit, which was in the midst of its very first capital campaign. The executive director, always looking to cut costs, took economy to a new level. Aside from insisting upon doing his own housekeeping, over the objections of his board chair, he was also positively obsessive about "recycling" (reusing) all of our photocopies and reports, citing "excessive" fundraising costs. My admonitions to shred these documents and accept the duplicating costs as a necessary cost of doing business went unheeded until, on one occasion during a leadership meeting, a principal donor and top volunteer to our campaign casually turned over the piece of paper on which she was taking notes to see a portion of her giving record and profile on the reverse side. This unfortunate incident finally made a believer out of the executive director. Diving to the bottom in cost is not always a prudent course of action. Although this incident was due to a lack of proper procedures rather than infrastructure, it is a clear demonstration of how many nonprofit organizations are only focused on immediate cost, not long-term benefit.

### *Practice Point*

*As a board member or other leadership volunteer, do you know the percentage of your organization's donor base that is actually solicited on at least an annual basis?*

*Do you know the manner in which constituent addresses are updated?*

*What method(s) does your organization use to determine financial abilities of your donors—a prospect review committee, electronic screening or both? Donor lists in your organization should be regularly reviewed, including the date of the last gift and the reason for giving, and this information should be used to inform a strategy for the next communication or solicitation.*

*Finally, what is the job description of the staff member(s) charged with managing the fundraising program? This role should be that of an active program manager with access to all levels of the organization, coordinating all of the moving pieces between board*

115

*members, the executive director, direct mail staff and gift recording clerks, along with all aspects of the organization. This role should not be filled by someone who is the chief party organizer, marketer—or worse—chief and sole solicitor.*

## What do donors want? How can I expand my organization through stewardship?

Simply stated, donors want to be asked to give, communicated with, thanked and have attention paid to them. Not too difficult, one would think. But these tasks are too often a jumble, with some of them getting done sporadically and clumsily, if at all. The effective execution and coordination of these tasks is the essence of what fundraising professionals call "stewardship," and it is the single most effective way to both grow and sustain your fundraising program. It is, however, an effort that is seen almost as an afterthought in many organizations. After all, it doesn't "pay." Remember, what donors really want is an experience that they cannot obtain anywhere else. Think about it.

**Donors want to be asked to give. They really do.**

Donors want to be asked to give. They really do. That being said, the single most oft-heard negative among donors is that they are asked—too often.[13] The second most heard complaint is that they are asked in an inappropriate manner. Donors want to be appropriately asked, and they will determine what is "appropriate." Need-based fundraising, alternatively, focuses on the organization's perceived urgent need without much regard to the timing or approach favored by the donor.

---

[13] The Cygnus Donor Survey." Cygnus Applied Research, Inc., 2010 and 2011.

Asking too often, or in the wrong manner, ——————————
is almost always the logical outcome of a fund **All donors want to**
development program that sees fundraising as **be appreciated.**
funding organizationally driven programs for **Some, but not**
organizationally determined needs. Remember **as many as you**
Principle 1: Donors are the Drivers—it's all **would think,**
about the donors. What is "too often" or "in- **want to be**
appropriate" will vary by donor. Take the time **recognized.**
and invest the effort to learn their differences. Donors will reward you
handsomely for learning this one skill well.

That being said, donors want to hear from you. Here again, it's
*what* donors want to hear. You don't know what donors want to learn
about your organization? Ask them. All donors want to be appreciated.
Some, but not as many as you would think, want to be recognized.
"Appreciation" and "recognition" are often confused…even by fundraising professionals. Appreciation is demonstrating to donors that they are
important to the ongoing success of your organization and that their
gifts are effective investments in the lives of others. Recognition is a
public acknowledgement of a donor or gift. If you're uncertain as to
what the donors really desire in terms of recognition, ask them. You
may be pleasantly surprised.

As you seek to divide your donors and potential donors into
meaningful groupings for your fundraising program, be aware of a
couple of misconceptions about the fundraising process. The first,
which was discussed earlier, is what I call "rounding up the usual
suspects." Organizations of all sizes fall victim to the thinking that
wealth is THE driver for fundraising. It is not. As we've seen before,
financial ability is necessary at some level, but it is not sufficient for a
successful program. The other common misconception about fundraising is what was previously referred to as "average giving." Remember

the "equal giving" illustration? "To raise $10,000," a board member says, "let's ask 100 individuals to give $100." We know that gifts are received in a variety of levels and follow some variation of the Pareto Principle of 80/20.

Regardless of how many times these ideas are shown to be little more than fundraising folklore, they continue to reappear in all sorts of nonprofit settings, both large and small.

### *Practice Point*

*What sort of stewardship or donor care program
is currently in place within your organization?
In process and protocol, does the program at least distinguish
between appreciation and recognition?*

*Do you know how often your donors are solicited and for what
purposes? You can construct a communications calendar grid
using the graphic on the next page. In doing so, you'll see the
solicitations very clearly. As you review this, use your gut instinct
to determine if you see too many solicitations—and remember,
a giving envelope in any communication, even an annual report,
counts as a "solicitation." Try to put yourself in the donor's
shoes, rather than approaching it from an organizational
perspective, which is too often a "we need money" perspective.*

### Why isn't fundraising a solution to a budget problem?

Although the wholesale comparison of fundraising to a for-profit business is neither exact nor appropriate, certain parallels are helpful as you build and implement a sustainable fundraising program. Look at transactional fundraising, which is an approach that uses fundraising

# Communication Calendar Grid

## (Communication occurrences by month versus constituency)

List method and content of every communication to each group and frequency.

| Constituency | January | February | March | April | May | June |
|---|---|---|---|---|---|---|
| A. Board Members | Letter (Example) | Email | Board Meeting | | | |
| B. Key Donors | Letter (Example) | Personal Visit | | | | |
| C. Mailing Lists | Event Invitation (Example) | Email | | | | |
| D. Potential Donors | Letter | Event Invitation | Email | | | |

| Constituency | July | August | September | October | November | December |
|---|---|---|---|---|---|---|
| A. Board Members | | | | | | |
| B. Key Donors | | | | | | |
| C. Mailing Lists | | | | | | |
| D. Potential Donors | | | | | | |

vehicles that depend upon some sort of material transaction. Transactional approaches include revenue-generating events, such as charity auctions and galas, as well as cause-related marketing programs, where a small portion of the purchase price of an unrelated good or service is donated by the merchandiser or manufacturer.

This approach to fundraising has a very short cash cycle, lasting only a quarter or less. It is very sensitive to price, hence the relatively low gift size. It is also dependent upon a high quantity of transactions, as there is a very low margin of net revenue to your organization. Such approaches must be delivered from scratch each time, as they do not engage the participants on a relational basis. "Brand loyalty," in this case, is virtually non-existent.

What sort of business employs a model that sounds a lot like this? You guessed it: it's the retail grocery industry. By employing transactional fundraising as your primary means of generating gift revenue, your organization is always in "low gear"—a lot of effort for very little return. Many nonprofit organizations, especially smaller ones, are in this mode of operation with their fundraising. Boards reinforce this approach—knowingly or unknowingly—by making current cash received the primary, if not sole, indicator of fundraising success. By de-emphasizing the relational aspect of philanthropy and not appreciating how donor commitment directly impacts his or her giving, well-intending board members see fundraising totals as just another number on the balance sheet.

For example, one organization's finance committee was hard at work developing a financial plan for the coming fiscal year. When a troublesome gap could not be filled by other revenue, the committee arbitrarily raised the fundraising goal for the coming year, as though simply raising the goal would translate into dollars. The question came up regarding which committee members would be increasing their annual gifts to meet this new, enlarged goal. In response, silence fell over the room. The committee quietly retreated from the new goal and set about looking at other alternatives to close the revenue gap.

The relational, sustainable approach to fundraising which generates renewable income over time, uses a considerably different business model. Unlike the cash-driven model, there is a great deal of time and effort invested in defining potential investors and learning their values and interests as they relate to your organization. Care is taken to compare the organization's mission statement to known investor values; in doing so, a "case" for support is created that has fundamental relevance with the potential investors. This "case" is used to construct communication instruments and gift solicitations that the donors of that particular organization will respond to, based upon values that are in concert with the organization's mission. A "custom product" is then developed for the donor (or customer, in the for-profit environment) with the expectation that the donor will grow with the organization, both in terms of relationship and the giving of numerous, and more significant, gifts over time.

A for-profit business model that closely resembles this significant, upfront investment in program and infrastructure, followed by the delivery of a customized product that will hopefully attract repeat customers, is the one employed by aircraft manufacturers. In the aircraft industry, as in investment philanthropy, customers (or donor investors) are acquired through considerable upfront expense with the initial sale; they are then continually and

> **Sustainable fundraising or development programs focus on long-term program investments and long-term donor relationships.**

competently nurtured for "repeat sales" of renewal parts, with only marginal additional cost to the supplier (or nonprofit).

Sustainable fundraising or development programs focus on long-term program investments and long-term donor relationships. Such programs produce the highest sustainable revenue over time. Sustainable fundraising programs are never a solution to a budget crisis due to the time they take to implement. They will, however, help prevent a future crisis from ever occurring.

## Practice Point

*If asked, can the board members of your organization enumerate the principal constituencies from which it derives direct, renewable support? Identifying these natural groups of potential supporters is a very important role of your governing board. What's more, your board should have adequate representation from these groups.*

---

### Currently at the Coeur d'Alene Center for the Arts

Lauren knows that there should be a more strategic and systematic connection between the various efforts to raise money for the center, but her lack of experience has tempered her willingness to step out and take risks by suggesting significant departures from current practice. After all, what the CACA has been doing all these years seems to work reasonably well. And yet, Lauren knows that there are a lot of potential donors and dollars that are just not being realized for the center.

Lauren's review of current programs revealed that the only fundraising effort that could justifiably be called an "acquisition program" is the direct mail piece that goes out in early spring to a list of non-donors; this list is largely comprised of the mass marketing mailing list that the CACA purchases each year from a general, direct marketing vendor. The profile that the vendor uses is rather generic and was set over ten years ago, when the original contract was signed. Nothing has changed since. The distribution list of the direct mail piece will occasionally include names that have come from a couple of other sources—names captured from participants in one of the center's programs or the occasional recommendation that comes via the "grapevine."

Existing donors do receive a separate mailing with slightly different wording, but it is essentially the same approach to all donors—prospective and otherwise—and it hasn't changed in message or appearance in five years. It works, after all. As to progressing donors to higher levels of giving, that's all up to them. Donors are asked each year for a gift...period. There is absolutely no effort to encourage them to give larger gifts, and there certainly isn't any assessment of their giving capacities. As to where each donor fits on a scale of commitment to the CACA, there is simply no indication, except in the rare case where a long-time donor has been quite purposeful in communicating that commitment. The existing fundraising software does have a donor-tracking feature, which is used to record the random communication when it comes to the attention of the center's staff and, occasionally, a board member. Although comments usually get recorded, they are never used.

This is not to say that the CACA has not been the beneficiary of some notable acts of generosity—it's just that staff and board members never know when they're coming. Bequests are always "unexpected," but of course, very welcome. That is, except for the bequest that carried the stipulation that the funds should be used to build a botanical garden in the area. Since there was no alternate use clause or latitude given to the center's leadership as to final use, that particular gift had to be declined. Except in the cases of Jacob Arnot and Harriet Simmons, the organization has never approached a donor to ask for a specific purpose.

The more Lauren ponders how to structure her plan, the more frustrated and confused she becomes. She has thought of hiring a fundraising consultant to help her sort things out, but the last time she suggested it, she was met with resistance; the potential cost has discouraged her from even broaching the idea with Jane. Lauren appreciates that "Rome wasn't built in a day," but she is uncertain which of the growth issues to tackle first. How can Principle 6: Divide & Grow help her as she puts together a fundraising plan for the organization?

## Questions to Consider

1.  How is a lack of awareness of Principle 6: Divide & Grow among the CACA staff and board members hampering the efforts to grow both the size and capacity of the center's donor base?

2.  Given Lauren's lack of experience and reluctance to suggest seeking outside expertise, what are the best first steps that she can take to begin to build a workable donor pipeline?

3.  What initial role(s) might the current board members assume in the process of restructuring fundraising efforts, if asked to do so?  Who should ask them?  How?  When?

4.  For the CACA, there are plenty of obstacles to successfully constructing a donor pipeline.  Can you identify some of those that lie buried in the center's path to systematic, sustainable fundraising?

# Principle 7

# Renew & Refresh

"Love me tender, love me sweet, never let me go."
— Elvis Presley

The date for the wedding is set. The bride, groom, parents, families and bridal party along with the supporting cast are in place. Since it was expected that old friends would decide to attend of their own volition, no formal invitations were mailed, but several "recruiters" were sent out walking the sidewalks of the city, handing out invitations to the ceremony as they went.

Finally, the day arrives. As the bride and groom take their places and the ceremony begins, a few old friends trickle in—the ones who, by chance, heard about the wedding at the last minute. There are even a few strangers who've shown up, presumably out of curiosity or to enjoy a good party at someone else's expense. The vast majority of those *expected* never come, however, since close friends were invited casually, if at all. As the couple says their vows and are declared husband and wife, they exit to half-hearted cheers from people who are just there for the event, not the wedding.

I don't know any couples who would organize their very important day this way, but many nonprofits do. Principle 7: Renew & Refresh is a guide to building loyalty and long-term benefits to a charitable organization, while adding new friends in a rational and manageable way.

## Why should I renew my donors?

This may seem like a rhetorical question. And it would be, except for the numbers of nonprofit organizations that put a great deal of attention on acquiring new donors, while devoting very little effort to keeping them in the fold. Whether you devote time and energy to retaining donors depends a lot on how you view them and what role they play in funding the organization.

In transactional fundraising, where buying and selling is the driver, donors are consumers. What they consume rarely, if ever, has any direct connection with your organization. Instead, the product or service exchanged is one that has general appeal, such as Hawaiian vacations or upscale gift baskets. Someone attending your fundraising event can easily obtain the same sort of enticement at another charity's event. The attendee's reason for attending the event will most likely have a tenuous connection to your organization's mission—if any. The motive is almost never a philanthropic one, as was illustrated earlier by the reporter's informal survey.

In such a fundraising program, there is the constant drive to sign up attendees for each event at the same or lower giving levels. Watching the RSVP list is often a real nail-biter for development officers and/or volunteers looking for "the numbers." And since no organizational loyalty is developed among those attending through these transactional vehicles, one starts from scratch each year. This sort of approach is like riding in a bike race and only using the low gear, with a 5 percent incline added for good measure. Responder fatigue sets in quickly. Since all responders are treated equally—that is, offered the same enticements at the same levels—giving expectations become arbitrarily low. Furthermore, their "thanks" is a generic gift, rather than a personal, individualized gesture. Competition from other organizations then becomes very real as transactional fundraising vehicles have a numbing sameness.

Income from transactional efforts generally plateaus within five years of the effort's inception. Income from this approach is also very sensitive to external economic conditions. During the most recent recession, I attended a gathering where the chief financial officer of a regional banking institution commented that area income from event-based fundraising was down 40 to 50 percent from pre-recession, "easy money," times.

By engaging donors on a direct basis and asking for donations based on your organization's mission and the work it does, you're already way ahead of other organizations that slog away chasing transactional revenue. That's because you have *donors,* not merely *responders.* Whether your organization's fundraising program will attain sustainability and derive the maximum benefit from these well-motivated individuals is largely dependent upon what you do with new donors after they walk through the door and identify themselves as such.

Individuals who make a first gift to your organization give modestly—and the term is relative to the individual's ability to give. Whether consciously or not, first-time donors want to "test" your organization and measure it against its stated mission. If they believe you're effective and successful, chances are that they will be *willing* to invest more heavily in your organization's future. The key word here is *willing.* Rare is the donor who, of his or her own volition, will give to the true measure of his or her financial ability without guidance and encouragement from your organization to do so. The form and substance of that guidance will determine whether your supporters will renew their giving year after year in ever increasing amounts, make only one gift or simply continue to make sporadic gifts at the "entry" level.

Renewing your donors and moving them toward truly commensurate giving is the key to sustainability. We've previously discussed that donors naturally divide themselves into groups related to affinity and ability. By renewing your organization's donors at a high rate, while moving them to giving levels that are commensurate with their individual financial abilities, your organization will achieve the oft-sought but elusive goal of a sustainable, expanding philanthropic revenue stream.

Nonprofits that do not focus on renewing donors and moving them to their highest levels of giving are often stuck in an ineffective, neverending cycle. An executive director once told me that his organization raised money using the "small gift model." I inquired as to just what that was. Essentially, the executive director believed that, by focusing only on small gifts, it would "broaden" the giving base, giving the organization both legitimacy and sufficient revenue. Noble perhaps, but seriously misguided. Remember 80/20? Another nonprofit organization used the approach of looking to a new group of potential supporters each year, believing that asking donors who have already given to give again is somehow inappropriate. Both of these organizations continue to struggle and remain on the fringes of the missions they are attempting to serve.

Organizations that are consumed with acquiring new donors devote very little attention to keeping them once they arrive. Once donors are lost, it is very difficult to return them to the fold. This tactic ends up "churning" donors, all giving at merely entry levels, with donors going out the back door almost as fast as they come in the front. This approach is simply not a sustainable strategy. By devoting serious energy to renewing its current donors, an organization's donor acquisition "problem" becomes a manageable one.

### *Practice Point*

*Assuming your organization keeps detailed records,
take a look at its "donor history," a comprehensive record of all
donors and gifts for each and every year. Now identify all of your
first-time donors from five years ago. Track their giving histories
coming forward, each year, to the present day. What do you see?
Look at gift size and gift giving consistency from year to year,
as well as your overall retention rate. Pay close attention to the
frequency and size of each particular donor's gifts from year to year.
Notice any patterns?*

*Among those donors who have remained with your organization
as loyal supporters, you're hopefully seeing a pattern of steadily,
perhaps modestly, increasing gifts for a sizeable majority of these*

131

*loyalists. (For those donors who don't stick around, that's a whole other issue.) You should also see significant gains in total giving coming forward each year for about 20 percent of your renewing donors. If you don't, you're missing out on perhaps the single largest piece of your current cash gift potential. This is the "cash piece" that you, as a board member, should be very aware of and focused on. By focusing on donor renewal and moving toward commensurate giving, you are on your way toward sustainability.*

---

### How do I get donors to renew—especially from the first to second year?

If renewal is the key to sustainability, how do you do it? I've mentioned that the most critical period for renewing a donor is the time between their first and second gifts to your organization. Although that is the period when renewal rates are often the lowest and deserve focused attention by your organization, the good news is that all donors need and want the same sort of attention and information from your organization to keep on giving—that is, to "renew."

> **The most critical period for renewing a donor is the time between their first and second gifts to your organization.**

Donor research has shown that the vast majority of donors will renew giving to your organization if you *consistently*—and that is the key word here—provide three things.[14] First, all donors want prompt and meaningful acknowledgment of their gifts to your organization. Both "prompt" and "meaningful" are value-laden terms and determined by the donor—not your organization. Suffice it

---

[14] "The Cygnus Donor Survey." Cygnus Applied Research, Inc., 2011.

to say that "prompt" is definitely something less than two weeks and that the required tax receipt is not sufficient to count as "meaningful" acknowledgment. Moreover, don't make the mistake of being so intent on "saving money" that included in the acknowledgment of a current gift is a giving envelope for *another* gift.

Second, donors—like investors—want to know that their investments will be used as they intended, or were led to believe they would be used, by your organization. Remember, it is the *perception* that trumps any reality here. What donors *perceive* about your organization is what is real—to them. Not that I recommend that you perform an artful bait-and-switch with your donors; I would rather that donor perceptions and your organization's actions be coincident with each other.

Third, remember that donors, like their investor counterparts in the for-profit world, are looking for results. Donors give to see positive change in a manner that is consistent with their personal values. In order to renew an investment, a donor needs to be made aware of these results *before* they are asked to give again. In designing donor communication programs, it is common for nonprofit organizations to pay particular and specific attention to their most loyal supporters. And why not? These are the individuals who truly *support* organizations. Thus, these stalwarts receive the "inside story," helping them to feel like part of the organization. If, however, you really want to make an impact on your first-time donor renewal rate—the most critical stage in donor renewal—why not provide all first-time donors with the inside story, too?

So, renewal of your donors is really rather simple. Provide the things that

> **Donors, like their investor counterparts in the for-profit world, are looking for results. Donors give to see positive change in a manner that is consistent with their personal values.**

donors have told you they want. Provide these things meaningfully and consistently, over time, and your organization will enjoy extremely high rates of renewal among its donors. I believe this is one of those "motherhood and apple pie" concepts that virtually every organization agrees with, when asked, but very, very few actually execute—certainly on a consistent basis. It's communicating what matters to the donor— and never failing to do so.

### Practice Point

*For years, fundraising professionals have held that the most up-to-date and "inside" information is reserved for an organization's very best supporters. Given the importance of renewing first-time donors, perhaps it's time to question that. Remember that the most critical time in a donor's relationship with your organization is that period between his or her first gift and the next gift solicitation. By making new donors feel like an important part of your organization, you raise the likelihood that they will become long-time investors.*

*Refer to your organization's most recent annual report. What do you see there? Hopefully, you don't see a giving envelope stapled into the spine. Also, are donors properly segregated according to type (individual, corporate, foundation)? Is there space given to memorial gifts? Are the overall financials of the organization included? Most importantly, are there compelling accounts of real-life outcomes that clearly demonstrate the transforming nature of gifts you have received in the last year?*

*What sorts of communication efforts does your organization mount for its first-time donors? Direct mail? Email? Personal letters? Personal telephone calls of thanks? Are your first-time donors brought into the "inner circle" of the organization quickly and completely, or must they work their way up the giving chart to the "founder's club" before getting frontline, insider information?*

## How can I refresh my donor base?

Even by doing all the right things all of the time, donor renewal rates will still be less than 100 percent. So, what's an organization to do? I mentioned before the need to have a formal donor acquisitions program as a part of your fundraising régime. Without such an effort, even the most vibrant organization will eventually ossify and become a fossil. And donor acquisition is about much more than new cash, or even the promise of it, into the organization. Adding new donors keeps the value-based lifeblood of your organization flowing. After all, philanthropy—sustainable philanthropy—is about relationships, not merely transactions. It is the "new blood" represented by new—and usually younger—donors that keeps the mission and purpose of your organization alive and relevant.

Since organized fundraising began, adding new donors has been about introducing new people to your program and purpose who have the financial ability and affinity to make an investment. Certainly, identifying new potential supporters is a primary fundraising task for board members. Reaching out to identifiable groups of individuals who have an affiliation with your organization of one kind or the other—members, patients, parents of students, alumni of one sort or the other, volunteers and vendors—should be an ongoing part of your effort to bring new donors into the fold. To expand to others who have values and goals similar to your organization's, the advent of tailored mass marketing is a boon. These tools have become extremely sophisticated in recent years and, when properly used, can be very effective.

The final answer to the question of refreshing and expanding your base is "all of the above." As we've seen throughout this discussion, *consistency* of effort is, perhaps, the most essential of the essential characteristics of a sustainable fundraising program.

Most organizations use a combination of leadership and staff networking, current donor referrals and some sort of mass marketing model to acquire new donors. Here again, the "inside out"—that is, beginning with those closest to you—is the most effective approach. Referrals will net more "real" prospective donors than mass marketing programs. Reaching beyond your known networks—which, by the way, are almost never fully utilized—will require some sort of mass marketing program. These programs are available from a number of qualified firms. They depend upon the development of a fairly accurate prospective donor profile; the profile is then applied to a data screening program, which will produce likely "suspects." These are then contacted and/or solicited through a combination of direct mail and email.

### Practice Point

*If you're new to the use of mass marketing mailing lists, take some time to carefully think about the profile of the individual that you want to reach with your message. In doing so, consider ability and affinity. Although any reputable vendor can assist you with the ability question, affinity can only be determined by you. Take a piece of paper and, in the next few minutes, quickly jot down a few characteristics of a "typical" supporter of your organization. Does any sort of clear picture emerge? You may have to ponder this one, but it's worth the effort.*

## Currently at the Coeur d'Alene Center for the Arts

For the attendees of the CACA's two primary, and several minor, fundraising events, the concept of "renewal" is an oxymoron. A small portion of the total attending are the predictable few that show up year after year, but their levels of financial participation are neither predictable nor consistent. Lauren knows that, every year, she essentially starts from scratch to plan and execute a successful art auction or gala.

Lauren's instinctive focus on renewal is where it should be—maintaining the small, loyal base of individual donors and adding to that base, over time. In the five years that Lauren has been with the organization, she has seen a small, but steady, decline in the year-to-year renewal rate of those loyal donors. For the most part, Lauren can chalk this decline up to donors either leaving the area or passing on—literally. Renewing long-time supporters doesn't seem to be an urgent issue; more disturbingly, Lauren has seen the slow, but noticeable, drop in the rate at which *first-time* donors are renewed for a second gift. The bottom line is that the CACA's program of individual giving is slowly, but surely, headed in the wrong direction.

The current direct mail solicitations, although they somewhat *segregate* long-time and first-time donors, don't really *discriminate* between the two groups. Lauren's past efforts to treat these groups differently haven't been met with a lot of enthusiasm. Neither Jane, the executive director, nor Dale, the board development committee chair, seem to understand the significance of truly distinguishing between these two groups; they can't seem to look past the additional cost of doing so. These trends are slow ones, but they're definitely headed in the wrong direction...and Lauren knows it.

Acknowledging gifts has been fairly standard and "routine" for a number of years. A tax receipt is sent within two weeks of receipt of the gift, and a personalized letter from the executive director follows four to six weeks thereafter. When Lauren became development director, she successfully persuaded Jane and the board to issue an annual report, providing a donor list and a few details about the center's activity for the previous year. It's not mailed to donors or prospective donors, however, but to the members of the chamber of commerce. This is because, at the conception of the idea of sending an annual report, a very active member of the chamber was then serving on the board. He felt that the best use of the CACA's budget was to distribute the report to business entities, as "we all know that business sponsorships for the fundraising events are where the action is." Even though this board member has since left the board, the habit remains.

In addition to donor communications, the timing of fundraising outreach, whether through events or direct mail gift solicitation, also hasn't changed much over time. Even with the summer art auction—the Art Extravaganza—occurring in the fourth quarter of the center's fiscal year and providing about 25 percent of their total revenue, no one seems to think that shifting the cash flow might be a prudent action to take.

Lauren attended a fundraising workshop last year, where she learned that approaching donors on a strategic and timely basis that is meaningful to them is quite effective in converting prospects and increasing the gift sizes of current donors. She shared the idea with Jane and Jack, the board chair, but was met with a yawn. At the time, things were going reasonably well, so why change what was working? Let's see how Principle 7: Renew & Refresh might help Lauren and the CACA.

## Questions to Consider

1. How are the CACA staff and board members ignoring Principle 7: Renew & Refresh?

2. How might the organization begin to adopt a more muscular approach to donor acquisition? How about donor renewal? Should they begin by focusing on acquisition or renewal?

3. Can you identify some simple efforts that would have minimal cost, but a significant effect, in acquiring new donors? What about renewals?

4. Perhaps more difficult than coming up with ideas to improve the CACA's acquisition and renewal programs would be selling them to the executive director and board members. How can Lauren create a sense of urgency for these needs, in the minds of the center's leaders?

# Principle

# Invest, Integrate & Evaluate

"Anything not worth doing well is not worth doing."
— Warren Buffett

E ach year in early January, the health clubs and fitness centers are crowded with those among us who have made the resolution to "get in shape" or "lose weight." And these fitness hopefuls really do want the results of regular exercise and proper diet. They want the results, but undergoing the process is quite a different matter. By April, most of these newly-resolved, energetic exercisers are nowhere to be seen. So it is with many who want to build a fundraising program that generates lasting, long-term benefits. Principle 8: Invest, Integrate & Evaluate is the principle of proper investment of time, energy and money along with a healthy dose of programmatic self-reflection.

### How should I invest time and resources into fundraising programs?

**I continue to see nonprofit organizations that behave as though fundraising is a cost-free undertaking.**

You've heard it before, "It takes money to raise money." And, although I have yet to find a board member, executive director or donor who would dispute this assertion, I continue to see nonprofit organizations that behave as though fundraising is a cost-free under-taking. Perhaps even worse is the view that a fundraising program will produce simply by applying money and time like buckshot—broadly and indiscriminately. The manner and level of financial investment in fundraising is, here again, largely determined by the fundraising philosophy and paradigm that your organization is operating from.

If your organization's decision makers see fundraising as a *transaction* between giver and receiver, they will invest its resources into fundraising along the same lines. The result will be extremely short time horizons, where the only real concern is cash coming in the door. It's all about current, spendable dividends, not capital growth.

If, on the other hand, your organization views fundraising as a strategic, long-term undertaking that encompasses both mission and investors, its approach will look fundamentally different. This is where many nonprofit organizations have difficulty moving forward and upward in their fundraising efforts. Once dependent upon current-use cash, it is often very difficult for the leadership to exhibit the focus, determination and stamina it takes to achieve long-term sustainability. Teach for America, Habitat for Humanity and even the Salvation Army all view fundraising as a strategic arm of the organization that is part and parcel to the organization's mission.

Recall the for-profit comparisons made in an earlier chapter. With the former, fundraising looks like the retail grocery industry. With the latter, fundraising more closely resembles the characteristics of aircraft design and manufacturing. Transactions are, by their very nature, "point-to-point." Fundraising built upon a transactional model sees a very "price sensitive" donor base with little or no loyalty, giving at marginally low rates, which can easily be deterred from discretionary giving by economic downturns—much like retail groceries. Like the retail grocery industry, broad-based success lies in relatively positive economic conditions and incredibly large volume.

Fundraising programs that are designed to build long-term relationships with their donors are, in many ways, very similar to the cash cycle and customer behavior of the aircraft design and manufacturing industry. Here, an aircraft designer and manufacturer conducts long-term design and testing efforts based upon real customer (donor) research, or donor research in a fundraising program at a considerable expense over a period of several years. This all occurs before even one airframe is offered for sale to the potential customer, or donor in the fundraising sense. Once the relationship with the customer is established through an initial sale, that sale often only

**Try convincing a board or executive director who is only focused on the cash coming in the door, to use the "aircraft approach."**

begins to amortize the true upfront cost of acquiring that customer. The value added by the customer, that which generates long-term, sustainable revenue at often increasing levels, is achieved through the return of a satisfied customer to purchase renewal parts (repeated gifts, over time) for an aircraft that has a life-span of a couple of decades.

Try convincing a board or executive director who is only focused on the cash coming in the door, to use the "aircraft approach." Although the promise of long-term success is there, short-term cash, even at subsistent levels, is often too intoxicating. I often see organizations devoting 70, 80, even 90 percent of their fundraising resources to develop 20 or 10 percent, sometimes less, of their potential revenue stream.

As a result of a focus on short-term fundraising approaches, many organizations go from meal to meal in a semi-starvation cycle. The paucity of infrastructure, especially with regard to fundraising in non-profit organizations, is well-documented.[15]

### *Practice Point*

*Take a look at your organization's fundraising budget for the past year, which should be distinguished from the one for general marketing and program promotion. Carefully analyze how money is spent on efforts to reach particular constituent types (individual, corporate or foundation) paying particular attention to the type of approach used with individuals (transactional or relational). Looking at the proportion of*

---

[15] Goggins, Ann and Howard, Don. "The Nonprofit Starvation Cycle." Stanford Social Innovation Review, 2009.

*expenditure, how closely do they compare with the national statistics on giving from individuals, corporations and foundations?[16] Although no organization perfectly mirrors the "norm," seeing how your organization compares nationally should generate some hard questions and perhaps facilitate a more comprehensive review of cost and benefit for your fundraising programs.*

## How do I remain consistent in my fundraising programs?

Consistency in effort, over time, will allow your organization to reach the highest levels of sustainable giving. Like the steam engine, the amount of energy applied to bring a cold boiler to its vapor point is considerable. Once steam is being generated, the energy necessary to keep the flywheel turning is greatly reduced. Allow the boiler to drop below the critical temperature, however, and considerably more energy is required. Likewise, consistency—doing the right things each and every year—is critical to achieving long-term fundraising success.

How do you achieve the high levels of consistency required? This is where a well-articulated plan, which is agreed upon, endorsed, executed and continually evaluated by the board and staff leadership, plays the starring role. That being said, lots of organizations have fundraising plans. While having a well-crafted plan, which is built upon the principles and assumptions of relational fundraising, is essential to sustainable success, it is not sufficient. It is in both planning and executing the plan that consistency is achieved. With an effective evaluation of your fundraising progress and programs, the plan is continually updated and funded in a strategic manner.

---

[16] National statistics on giving can be found through the Giving USA Foundation, which releases an annual giving report; visit http://www.givingusareports.org/.

## How do I integrate a sustainable program?

Achieving the benefits of a sustainable fundraising program is largely dependent on how well you integrate the various components of your program. Recalling Principle 1: Donors are the Drivers, such integration is achieved through the construction of a seamless donor pipeline. No, I'm not suggesting that you put your donors in one end and push them out the other like sausage.

What we want to achieve is an integration among your various fundraising vehicles that, from the donor's point of view, is seamless. As the donor "progresses" from giving small cash gifts to cash gifts reflective of his or her financial ability, on to gifts of assets and, ultimately, gifts which are deferred or estate in nature, the donor's needs and desires must be handled in a manner that is structured and directed but not obsequious. To the donor, such interaction with your organization appears natural and almost effortless. On the inside, the program is a well-tuned machine with very low tolerance for unwanted variances.

A few years back, I was asked to give a presentation to the board of a liberal arts college in the Northeast. As the meeting adjourned and I walked out of the building into the pleasant spring air, one of the board members came alongside me and engaged me in conversation. The board member asked me a couple of questions related to the presentation, and then he made an offhand comment that took me briefly aback. "I used to think all of you guys were just a lot of showmen," the board member intoned, "until I learned about the machine that is behind you." This board member understood that successful development requires the consistent, fine-tuned effort that, to the outside observer, looks almost effortless due to the precision-focused organization operating on the inside. Fundraising programs that sustain themselves through renewable and expandable income exhibit an almost fanatical attention to detail and consistency, on the part of the staff administering them.

A perception of total care and concern by the donor on the part of the organization is largely won or lost in the details.

Development offices are like any other. Without a cogent, over-arching plan and strong leadership, fundraisers will act independent of each other and see the goal of a particular program as being separate and distinct from the other fundraising efforts. This "everyone on their own track" approach is quite prevalent among fundraising offices, both large and small. Development officers are sometimes given produc-tivity goals that don't account for the integrated nature of fundraising and the three- to five-year business cycle. Board members get into the act, as well, by focusing on cash received since the last meeting.

This tendency to view fundraising as smaller, independent processes is often reinforced and rewarded by the criteria selected and the methods used to evaluate fundraising programs. Too often, the annual fund has goals that are independent of the high-cash program, which is independ-ent of the major gift program, which has no connection to the planned giving effort. Essentially, "the left hand doesn't know what the right hand is doing." The result is fundraising outreach that appears sporadic and even overbearing to the donor.

The keys to integrating fundraising programs and obtaining a "seamless" program delivery at the highest possible levels are simply to (1) employ Principle 1: Donors are the Drivers, in any overarching plans and (2) set objectives for each individual effort so that they co-ordinate, rather than conflict, with the overall program goals.

### *Practice Point*

*Want to get an idea of how "seamless" your handling of donors really is? Take a random sample of five to ten long-time donors (people who have been involved with your organization for a minimum of five years). Call them and start by thanking them for their loyalty and commitment, as well as mentioning how their gifts are involved in the outstanding work your organization does. Then, ask if the solicitations they are receiving communicate the organization's needs while speaking to their interests. It can be tough to get a totally unbiased answer as no one generally wants to be the bearer of bad news. Because of this, you may want to consider having this sort of survey designed and executed by a qualified independent party or consultant.*

### What criteria should I use to measure success?

In almost all of the fundraising operations I have seen, there is an overfocus on cash received (usually in the previous quarter and some-times in the last fiscal year) as the leading indicator of success. Don't get me wrong; cash is important. It's very important. That is, after all, what we are hoping to increase. Cash, however, is a fairly poor indicator of fundraising program effectiveness and success, as well as an especially poor predictor of future performance. Cash is the result, not the cause, of doing the right things consistently.

**Cash is the result, not the cause, of doing the right things consistently.**

So, what should you be watching for and evaluating in your fundraising program? First, remember that fund development has a fairly lengthy business cycle—three to five years for a program that includes cash, high-end cash, major and deferred giving components. Thus, cash receipts need to be placed into the larger context of the program, which is then evaluated over at least a three- to five-year period. Better evaluators of your program's effectiveness and predictors of future success are found in the Eight Principles.

The Sustainable Fundraising Matrix on the following page gives three key benchmarks for each of the Eight Principles; using these benchmarks, you can assess the overall effectiveness of your organization's fundraising and pinpoint where things can be improved. By doing so, you can focus your efforts on the areas that truly need attention.

Start by giving a realistic appraisal of your organization using the Score Card on page 151. It's a simple "1, 2, 3" scoring system. For each benchmark, evaluate whether your organization is just "starting" to move in the direction of a particular benchmark (1 point), "in progress" (2 points) or "totally there" (3 points). If your organization doesn't meet a benchmark at all, then give yourself a "0" for that particular benchmark. After assigning a score for each of the 24 benchmarks, total up your points.

Very few charitable organizations can realistically come close to a perfect score of 72. If, after an honest self-evaluation, your organization scores at **least 50 points**, then the principles of sustainable fundraising are "alive and well" and being consistently employed. In all likelihood, your organization's fundraising bottom-line is reasonably stable and perhaps even expanding over time. Continue to do what you're doing right—and address the areas of weakness—and your organization is sure to flourish.

If your organization scores **between 25 and 50 points**, then it's headed in the right direction. At this point, you probably haven't reached some of the hallmarks of sustainable fundraising, such as high donor renewal rates, consistent major gifts and a predictable stream of deferred and planned gift commitments. In restructuring your processes to ensure productivity, pay attention to the lower scoring benchmarks, with this book as a guide to help refocus your efforts.

# The Sustainable Fundraising Matrix

1 = Starting     2 = In Progress     3 = Totally There

| Principle | Benchmark *1* | Benchmark *2* | Benchmark *3* |
|---|---|---|---|
| Donors are the Drivers | Is the average gift of your established donors steady or increasing on an annual basis? | Is the percentage of income from all transactional fundraising 20 percent or less of your total fundraising revenue? | Is the percentage of non-donor prospects who become first-time donors after being asked steady or increasing? |
| Begin at the Beginning | Do your program and outreach outcomes validate your mission statement? | Have you obtained third-party research of your donors' attitudes and perceptions of your organization and its efforts? | Do you have mechanisms for accepting, and responding to, self-initiated donor feedback? |
| Leadership Leads | Do all of your board members make a gift from their personal resources each year? | Do all of your board members participate in some phase of the fundraising process? | Does your board conduct an annual self-evaluation of both the board as a whole and individual member performance? |
| Learn & Plan | Do you have an annual fundraising plan that is board-approved and properly resourced? | Do you know the top five reasons your donors support you? | Do you know the five largest natural groups of donors that support you? |
| Work from the Inside Out | Do your board members make annual gifts that are commensurate with their individual abilities? | Do you have a staff giving program that is healthy and growing? | Are volunteers asked for gifts? |
| Divide & Grow | Do you have a fundraising program that is specifically designed to acquire new donors? | Are all of your donors internally assigned "ability" and "affinity" designations? | Are your donors being actively progressed in the pipeline according to their ability and affinity designations? |
| Renew & Refresh | Do you know the percentage of first-time donors that make a second gift? Is that percentage steady or increasing? | Do you have a well-developed program of thanking donors in ways that are meaningful to them? | Are solicitations timed and delivered strategically according to your donors' preferences? |
| Invest, Integrate & Evaluate | Is your fundraising program rationally resourced—that is, are resources sufficient to meet goals? | Do the various goals for your fundraising efforts coordinate rather than compete? | Do you conduct an annual formal review of your fundraising program that involves both staff and board? |

# Are You in the League?

**Total Score** _____

## Perfect Score: 72

This chart is a simple way to get a handle on how closely your organization approaches the sustainable fundraising ideal. There are obviously nuances to every situation, so consider this tool one that provides the "rule of thumb." Still, as a board member, volunteer or professional fundraiser, it will be very useful in helping you focus on the variables that are truly indicative of long-term growth and stability. A more detailed description of score results can be found within Principle 6: Divide & Grow.

**Scoring:**

50+     Consistently winning seasons are in sight

25-50    In the league and moving up

0-25     Not yet in the league—you need to rethink your game strategy

Organizations scoring **less than 25 points** exhibit very few of the characteristics of a sustainable program—that is, stable income expanding relatively consistently over time. Your organization is likely saddled with high fundraising costs, experiencing considerable volatility in net revenue and may have leadership boards whose members are reluctant to make yearly, commensurate gifts. Hiring a knowledgeable consultant and facilitator to evaluate your organization's weak spots and offer suggestions is probably a good idea at this point.

## *Practice Point*

*Once you have completed the matrix for your organization, take some time to review the individual benchmark scores. Do you see any patterns? After reviewing your scores, identify the three strongest benchmarks for your organization. Then, hone in on the three that are the weakest. Can you identify some initial steps you might take to begin addressing these?*

### Currently at the Coeur d'Alene Center for the Arts

As Jane and Lauren work to finalize their revised operating and fundraising plans for the September board meeting, the issue of budget begins to loom large. In the past, approving the operating budget has been relatively easy; with programming more or less set, there has been very little change from year to year. The fundraising budget has consisted primarily of funds for all mailings, the annual report, the purchase of the outside mailing list and software renewals. All of the fundraising events are seen as "pay as you go" and are expected to be self-financing.

With the revenue downturn from the most recent summer art auction—the Art Extravaganza—coupled with the desire to invest in new and expanded efforts focused on individual giving, both Lauren and Jane can almost feel the earth beginning to move beneath them. They both wonder what they should tackle first. How can they bring staff and board together? Any way you look at it, there is going to be pain—both emotional and financial.

Until now, there hasn't been much interest in coordinating

any of the CACA's various fundraising efforts—they each pretty much stand alone. After all, they raise money, don't they? Flush times have been a blessing for the center, but they have also served as a sedative. Now the nap is over.

Lauren sensed the center was traveling without a good fundraising road map but up until now hasn't been able to convince anyone else that they needed a solid plan. During the past few weeks, however, Jane's attitude toward Lauren's urgings has moved from "ho hum" to "you may have a real point here." Lauren at least believes that she has Jane's ear on the issue. But what about Dale, the development committee chair of the board? Jack, the board chair has been eager to get moving— could this become the "hot issue" he has been hoping for to consolidate his leadership?

Perhaps the place to start is to get staff and board members involved in a serious review and evaluation of the current fundraising efforts. Although it's been mentioned from time to time, such a review has never been done. The response was always, "Why tinker with what works?"

To be fair, the board reviews the fundraising cash received totals every quarter, which they compare to the same period in the previous year. Since cash from all fundraising sources is grouped together for these reports, it's not immediately clear to a board member reviewing these reports exactly how the cash parses out. And with revenues being relatively constant over time, few board members have asked. Revenue from ticket sales, enrollments and the ongoing membership program are separated, however, and there have been occasions when these trends have been hotly debated by the board.

How might Lauren and Jane develop a thorough plan, win over the board and staff, and move the organization in a new and sustainable direction? Let's see how Principle 8: Invest, Integrate & Evaluate might help them in doing so.

## Questions to Consider

1. How would you evaluate the CACA's efforts regarding Principle 8: Invest, Integrate & Evaluate?

2. Jane and Lauren have a number of significant decisions to make in the next couple of weeks; how might they prioritize them?

3. Which, if any, of the fundraising issues that face the center should Jane and Lauren be prepared to "go to the floor" on?

4. How might Jane and Lauren build support for their recommended changes in order to achieve an actionable consensus among both the staff and board?

# What are the main points and questions from each of the principles to consider as I evaluate my organization?

### Principle 1: Donors are the Drivers.

What are your donors telling you? Look at their behavior. What is your donor renewal rate, especially for first-time donors? Look at the average gift size in your annual or operating cash appeal. Is it increasing, decreasing or staying the same? What is your rate of "converting" potential donors into actual donors? You can even separate your potential donor list into groups to look at your program more closely.

### Principle 2: Begin at the Beginning.

Take a close look at your mission statement and fundraising case for support. You'll recall that your "case" is the document that provides rationale as to why prospective donors should support what you do, why they should support you now and why you're the organization to accomplish the task. Is there real congruence here? Does it still speak to your organization's mission? When was the last time you had these documents evaluated by a qualified consultant? What are donors telling you about your case? Ask them. Conduct informal surveys in-house or engage an unaffiliated professional to thoroughly examine your donors' level of understanding and reaction to your case.

### Principle 3: Leadership Leads.

How healthy is your board giving? Are your board members giving at levels commensurate with their individual financial abilities? Are they participating in identifying new donors, cultivating donors and stewarding donors? Are your board members approving annual fundraising plans with realistic budgets, thereby giving your organization the resources and ability to raise money? Many organizations find it helpful to have the board undergo an evaluation, both as a whole and individually, each year. Getting a consultant or other outside facilitator to conduct this can be worth the ticket price.

## Principle 4: Learn & Plan.

Do you have an annual fundraising plan in place that truly makes sense for your organization and donors? Do you truly know why your donors support you? What are the top five natural groupings of donors that support you?

## Principle 5: Work from the Inside Out.

How many of your staff members make regular gifts? Volunteers? Are you building relationships with those who are closest to your organization? Are they partners in the fundraising process, rather than merely givers?

## Principle 6: Divide & Grow.

Have you identified the natural groupings that supporters fall into? What does your program infrastructure look like? Does it match the needs and desires of your supporters? Is it sufficient enough to serve them?

## Principle 7: Renew & Refresh.

What is your first-time donor renewal rate? How close to capacity are your donors giving? What are the movement rates between each of your fundraising programs (e.g., cash to high-end cash, high-end cash to gifts of assets)? At the end of the day, it really is all about renewal and acquisition—with a strong emphasis on renewal.

## Principle 8: Invest, Integrate & Evaluate.

What are the costs of the various appeals of your program? Are they too high? Are they too low? Do the various fundraising goals complement or compete? Is there a formal, comprehensive review of your overall development program annually? Is it used to inform the next year's plan?

Once you've evaluated where your organization stands, it's only a matter of "filling in the holes," right? Well, maybe. Remember, being successful in establishing a sustainable fundraising program is about doing the right things—and doing them consistently. Many organizations set out with good intentions but, for whatever reasons, fail to achieve the expected level of success. Often, this is simply because they didn't stick to it long enough or grew complacent after some initial success. It doesn't have to be that way, though.

### Coeur d'Alene Center for the Arts: An Epilogue

This case study is intentionally left open-ended. And while there is no "solution" or "right answer," there are several possible outcomes—some positive and others negative. Furthermore, some key facts are implied, rather than explicit. As with any drama, real or fictional, there is a certain amount of "reading between the lines" that is required. One such example is what may seem to be an apparent disconnect between executive director Jane's desire to move away from transactional fundraising, while having an initially tepid reaction to some of Lauren's recommendations.

Jane is like a lot of us. She wants the result, but she's not sure she wants to endure the process. She even shows ambivalence toward adopting a strong donor focus, as demonstrated by her desire to get the program director on board with the need for change...rather than just taking the initiative herself. Yet, she reacts sharply to Lauren's suggestion that the center's donors really aren't that in love with the current programming.

Lauren is very typical of many development professionals. She has good instincts but is a bit short on experience, while feeling as though she has great responsibility without a lot of authority. While fundraising is an art and a science, it is *art* that comes from the "gut." Lauren will, hopefully, go with her instincts, which are rarely off base in fundraising.

Jack is like a lot of board members. He comes from outside the nonprofit arena, but has been successful in a profession where he can control most of the variables. He's competent and has the makings of an excellent board chair. He, too, is trying to find his way.

*Let's look at a possible outcome of our fictional*
*Coeur d'Alene Center for the Arts:*

Lauren has developed a fundraising plan that seeks to preserve the two transactional events more or less in their present form for the next three years. During that period, she is recommending a significant effort to develop and enlarge the existing individual donor base. Prior to the meeting, she sought the support of Jack, the board chair, and the two were able to convince Jane that moving ahead aggressively was worth the risk. The clincher for Jane was that Jack offered to personally donate 50 percent of the additional funding needed to get the new individual effort off the ground, and to conduct a vigorous annual campaign among the board members to fund the other half. Luckily for the CACA, Lauren was able to ignite Jack's passion and demonstrate how his leadership could make the critical difference.

*Three years later...*

The first thing you notice about the center's fundraising program is how "of one mind" the board is regarding fundraising. That didn't come easily. When Jack threw down the gauntlet three years prior, the reaction of the members of the board was to be expected. About a third of those on the board were whole-heartedly in favor and had seemingly been waiting for someone to step forward. Another third understood the need and participated. The remaining third felt they were being imposed upon and that nothing really needed to change. This group quietly, and voluntarily, removed themselves from leadership during the first year of the new fundraising program.

Currently, three years after the initial meeting, there are still events, although the revenue-generating aspect is less important. A few new events have been added, with the specific purpose of building donor relationships. Most importantly, the individual donor base has expanded by about 20 percent and the cash received in the annual giving program is up 35 percent. Lauren has been working with a select few of the donors, who she believes will be the first to make major gifts to the center.

If the center continues to strengthen its relational fundraising program through consistent application of the Eight Principles, its base of support will continue to broaden and deepen, becoming less subject to external economic forces.

# Coming Full Circle

Let's return to the fearless Marine who went weak-kneed while asking the frail, elderly woman for a gift. Remember him? David had every right to be confident in seeking a gift from the woman in question. He had made his own gift, he passionately believed in the project and he knew that she had both the inclination and capability to participate in a project that would benefit the entire community. Yet, despite all of these factors, he found himself looking at the floor as he asked for her support. Why?

In David's case, he had very good intentions and had taken many of the steps necessary for success. What he lacked, however, was the firm conviction that she *needed* and *wanted* something he could offer. Despite his strong support of the project, he initially saw the gift solicitation as one-way—a sale, rather than a mutually beneficial opportunity.

Donors are looking for an opportunity to invest—they really are. When the formidable woman told David that she liked to be "looked in the eye" when asked to invest, he immediately understood what had been lacking in his approach. The good news is that he had the self-confidence to correct his mistake and move forward.

With a little coaching and encouragement, he not only obtained a sizable commitment to the project, but he made a life-long friend for the organization he represented. He also became the most successful fundraiser (investment counselor) the organization ever had. It was my pleasure to have worked with him and to have seen the project become a reality.

David's anxiety was transformed into a priceless opportunity—for both him and the donor. I know because he told me. I'm telling you now—you can make this happen too.

# Suggested Reading
# & Additional Resources

## Suggested Reading

Bassoff, Michael and Chandler, Steve. *RelationShift: Revolutionary Fundraising.* San Francisco: Robert D. Reed Publishers, 2001.

Bremner, Robert H. *American Philanthropy.* Chicago: The University of Chicago Press, 1988.

Brooks, Arthur C. *Who Really Cares: The Surprising Truth About Compassionate Conservatism.* New York: Basic Books, 2006.

Burk, Penelope. *Donor Centered Fundraising: How to Hold on to Your Donors and Raise Much More Money.* Chicago: Cygnus Applied Research, Inc., 2003.

Collins, Jim. *Good to Great and the Social Sectors: Why Business Thinking Is Not the Answer.* Boulder, CO: Jim Collins, 2005.

Covey, Stephen R. *The Seven Habits of Highly Effective People.* New York: Simon & Schuster, 1989.

Crutchfield, Leslie R. and Grant, Heather McLeod. *Forces for Good.* San Francisco: Jossey-Bass, 2008.

Cullman, Lewis B. *Can't Take it With You: The Art of Making and Giving Money.* Hoboken, NJ: John Wiley & Sons, 2004.

Cullman, Lewis B. *How To Succeed in Fundraising By Really Trying.* www.LewisCullman.com, PDF.

De Tocqueville, Alexis. *Democracy in America.* Richard D. Heffner (Ed.). New York: Alfred A. Knopf, 1994.

Drucker, Peter F. *Managing the Nonprofit Organization.* New York: Harper, 2006.

Gaudiani, Claire with Burnett, David. *Generosity Rules! A Guidebook to Giving*. Lincoln, NE: iUniverse, 2007.

Gaudiani, Claire. *The Greater Good: How Philanthropy Drives the American Economy and Can Save Capitalism*. New York: Holt, 2004.

Heath, Chip and Heath, Dan. *Switch: How to Change Things When Change Is Hard*. New York: Broadway Books, 2010.

La Piana, David. *The Nonprofit Strategy Revolution: Real-Time Strategic Planning in a Rapid Response World*. Saint Paul: Fieldstone Alliance, 2008.

Lakey, Berit M. *The Board Building Cycle*. Washington, D.C.: BoardSource, 2007.

Levy, Reynold. *Yours for the Asking: An Indispensable Guide to Fundraising and Management*. Hoboken, NJ: John Wiley & Sons, 2008.

Lord, James Gregory. *The Raising of Money: Thirty-Five Essentials Every Trustee Should Know*. Cleveland: Third Sector Press, 1983.

Maxwell, John C. *The 21 Irrefutable Laws of Leadership: Follow Them and People Will Follow You*. Nashville: Thomas Nelson, 1998.

Rosso, Henry A. *Achieving Excellence in Fundraising* (3rd ed.). Eugene R. Tempel et al. (Eds.). San Francisco: Jossey-Bass, 2011.

Rosso, Henry A. *Rosso on Fundraising: Lessons from a Master's Lifetime of Experience*. San Francisco: Jossey-Bass, 1996.

Schervish, Paul G., et. al. *Taking Giving Seriously*. Indianapolis: Indiana University Center on Philanthropy, 1993.

Sinek, Simon. *Start With Why: How Great Leaders Inspire Everyone to Take Action*. New York: Portfolio, 2009.

## Additional Resources

The Association for Healthcare Philanthropy (AHP), www.ahp.org

Association of Fundraising Professionals (AFP), www.afpnet.org

BBB Wise Giving Alliance, www.give.org

BoardSource, www.boardsource.org

The Center on Philanthropy at Indiana University, www.philanthropy.iupui.edu

Center on Wealth and Philanthropy at Boston College, www.bc.edu/research/cwp

Charity Channel, www.charitychannel.com

Charity Navigator, www.charitynavigator.com

The Chronicle of Philanthropy, www.philanthropy.com

Council for Advancement and Support of Education (CASE), www.case.org

Giving Institute, www.givinginstitute.org

GuideStar USA, Inc., www.guidestar.com

National Council of Nonprofit Associations, www.ncna.org

Partnership for Philanthropic Planning (PPP), www.pppnet.org

The Philanthropy Roundtable, www.philanthropyroundtable.org

# Acknowledgements

"Without counsel plans go wrong,
but with many advisors they succeed."
—Proverbs 15:22

Any achievement, no matter how singular it may appear, is the result of the effort, wisdom and counsel of many. So it is with *The Eight Principles of Sustainable Fundraising*. Throughout my career in fundraising, I have been privileged to work with several outstanding professionals, mentored by some of the best and continually benefit from the experience and wisdom of the many donors whom I have come to know.

My fundraising career began with Ketchum, Inc., one of the founding members of the American Association of Fundraising Counsel. While there, I was mentored by the late Robert J. Simonds, former executive vice president whose professionalism and "heart" for the business I still revere and Lawrence Weber, retired former president. Ketchum's strong emphasis on peer counsel allowed me to learn much from colleagues Mary Doorley Simboski, Robert Demont and David Aiken.

After moving into higher education, I came to know and appreciate the team at Benz, Whaley, Flessner. I count Bill Lowery and Bobbi Strand, former principals, as both counselors and friends. Bruce Flessner, a current principal, unwittingly gave me the idea of developing the comparison between fundraising and the aircraft industry in a talk he gave eight years ago.

Chris Bryant, the most astute and professional executive recruiter I know, gave me the opportunity to come to Idaho and to him I am deeply grateful. Upon arriving in Idaho, Bill Drake, chairman of Drake Cooper, became—and continues to be—a source of tremendous guidance and support. I remember fondly, our lunch when the idea of M.E. Grace was born.

During the past four years since M.E. Grace's founding, so many individuals have provided guidance and support. Barbara Bowman, vice president for ministry advancement at Mission Aviation Fellowship; Jennifer Deroin, branch president of Intermountain Community Bank; Rick Youngblood, regional president of Intermountain Community Bank; Lynn Hoffman, executive director of the Idaho Nonprofit Center; Katie Mooney and Jenna Haener of Valice, my "web whizzes;" and Justin Foster, my source of all things GenY.

I thank Penelope Burk, whose talk in Boise two years back sparked the initial idea for this book. I am sincerely grateful for the insightful and honest input of several colleagues including Stuart Weiser, CFRE, vice president of development, marketing and communications, Idaho Youth Ranch; Jim Everett, CEO of Treasure Valley YMCA; Chris Taylor, CEO of Fisher's Document Systems; and long-time friend Lee Royce, president of Mississippi College.

Members of the Idaho Chapter of the Association of Fundraising Professionals, including Beth Markley and Autumn Kersey have also played their role.

I have been the beneficiary of tremendous talent in the preparation of this volume. This book would simply not be a reality had it not been for the unswerving encouragement and dedication of Maryanna Young of Aloha Pubishing, and my editor, Stacy Ennis. I offer them my heartfelt thanks.

Larry C. Johnson
Founder, M.E. Grace & Asscociates

# About The Author

Larry C. Johnson, CFRE, has over twenty years of direct involvement with charitable fund development and nonprofit management, with fourteen of those years at the senior executive level. Passionate in helping nonprofits achieve the highest levels of sustainable funding, Larry has enabled a number of fund development and institutional advancement programs move to the next level of excellence.

A graduate of both Vanderbilt and Yale Universities, Larry's career began in Fortune 100 program management before moving into charitable fundraising with Ketchum, Inc., as fundraising counsel. Larry subsequently served as chief advancement officer for four colleges and universities before founding M.E. Grace in 2007 with a mission to help nonprofits appreciate their true fundraising potential and show them how to achieve it. As a consultant, Larry has served over 50 institutional clients, working with the staff, volunteers and boards of nonprofits in education, the arts, youth, community service, health care and faith-based organizations.

Larry is a frequent speaker and trainer and has led workshops, seminars and conferences for the Council for the Advancement of Education (CASE), the Association of Fundraising Professionals (AFP), the Idaho Hospital Association, the Idaho Nonprofit Center, the Boise Metro Chamber of Commerce, Intermountain Community Bank, Panhandle State Bank and Clear Rock Capital. Larry was named the Outstanding Development Executive in Idaho for 2010 by AFP.

A long-time advocate of sustainable philanthropy as an essential component of a healthy and stable society, Larry holds the Certified Fundraising Executive (CFRE) distinction. He is a member of the Association of Fundraising Professionals (AFP), the Partnership for

Philanthropic Planning and BoardSource, as well as serves on the board of the Southwest Idaho Planned Giving Council.

Larry lives near Boise, Idaho where he and his wife, Connie, devote time to exploring the Rockies on horseback, hiking in the Sawtooths and backcountry skiing. An amateur outdoor photographer of the West, he also enjoys seeking out new locales astride his Harley.

*How can your fundraising become out of the box?*

*Who else needs to be involved for your fundraising to be a success?*